VOLUME 2

BY
CLAMP

HAMBURG // LONDON // LOS ANGELES // TOKYO

RG Veda Vol. 2
created by CLAMP

Translation - Haruko Furukawa
English Adaptation - Christine Schilling
Copy Editor - Aaron Sparrow
Retouch and Lettering - William Suh
Production Artists - James Dashiell, Eric Pineda, & Jason Milligan
Cover Design - Jorge Negrete

Editor - Carol Fox
Digital Imaging Manager - Chris Buford
Pre-Press Manager - Antonio DePietro
Production Managers - Jennifer Miller and Mutsumi Miyazaki
Art Director - Matt Alford
Managing Editor - Jill Freshney
VP of Production - Ron Klamert
President and C.O.O. - John Parker
Publisher and C.E.O. - Stuart Levy

A  Manga

TOKYOPOP Inc.
5900 Wilshire Blvd. Suite 2000
Los Angeles, CA 90036

E-mail: info@TOKYOPOP.com
Come visit us online at www.TOKYOPOP.com

ISBN: 1-59532-485-2

First TOKYOPOP printing: July 2005

10 9 8 7 6 5 4 3 2 1

Printed in the USA

ZENMI CASTLE,
TOURITEN

HEAVEN'S MANDATE HAS CALLED FOR THE GATHERING OF THE SIX STARS. AND THEY HAVE ALREADY BEGUN TO ASSEMBLE AROUND THE ORPHAN CHILD OF LORD ASHURA AND THE REBEL KING, LORD YASHA.
WHEN ALL SIX ARE IN THEIR HANDS, YOUR PRECIOUS TENKAI WILL BE TAKEN FROM YOU.
SEI-DEN
聖伝
STORM OF THE SIX STARS I

I DON'T KNOW WHAT THE HELL THESE SIX STARS ARE ALL ABOUT, BUT...
...I DON'T GET WHY YOU'RE BOTHERING US ABOUT ALL THIS. LORD YASHA IS UNDER YOUR RULE, AFTER ALL, BISHAMONTEN.
YEAH. 'SIDES, THEY'RE JUST SOME BABY AND A KING THAT LOST HIS WHOLE TRIBE...YOU TOO PUSSY TO HANDLE EVEN WEAKLINGS LIKE THEM, BISHAMONTEN?
ZOUCHOUTEN AND KOUMOKUTEN, WATCH YOUR LANGUAGE. HAVE YOU FORGOTTEN YOU ARE IN THE KING'S PRESENCE?
IT'S ALL RIGHT, BISHAM-ONTEN.

GENERAL OF THE SOUTHLAND, ZOUCHOUTEN.
GENERAL OF THE WESTLAND, KOUMOKUTEN.
AND GENERAL OF THE NORTHLAND, BISHAMONTEN.
BRING ME THE HEADS OF ASHURA AND YASHA.
THOUGH YOU TWO SHOULD KNOW NOT TO TAKE THEM LIGHTLY. AFTER ALL, THEY'VE LIVED THIS LONG.
AND HAVING FAILED TO GET RID OF THEM ALL THIS TIME... YOU ARE STILL A DISGRACE TO ME.

OH MY, EVERYONE'S HERE... WHAT'S THE OCCASION?
SHASHI, YOU DON'T USUALLY COME DOWN TO THE THRONE ROOM.
I JUST CAME HERE TO SEE HOW YOU'RE DOING, MY DARLING.
IT'S BEEN A WHILE, FATHER.
AH, MY QUEEN. MAY I INQUIRE AS TO HOW YOU ARE FEELING TODAY?
NO, YOU MAY NOT.

"ASHURA" STILL LIVES? WELL, I NEVER! IT MAKES ME DOWNRIGHT SICK KNOWING THAT HE'S STILL BREATHING!
THAT ABOMINATION OF A CHILD...THE VERY THOUGHT OF HIM MAKES MY SKIN CRAWL!
I DIDN'T KNOW YOU COULD HATE YOUR OWN OFFSPRING THAT MUCH...LET ALONE ONE FROM YOUR SET OF TWINS.
ANYWAY, JUST LEAVE IT TO US, SIRE. ASHURA AND YASHA CAN'T ESCAPE US...
WE'RE THE FOUR GODS AFTER ALL.
DEATH TO THOSE WHO DEFY THE GOD KING.
I APPRECIATE YOUR LOYALTY.

THE NERVE OF THAT WOMAN!
WHO DOES SHE THINK SHE IS, TALKING TO US LIKE THAT?! TALK ABOUT BEING ON YOUR HIGH HORSE!
IT WAS ONLY WHEN SHE MARRIED INTO THE ASHURA TRIBE THAT SHE WENT FROM BEING A MEASLY "HUMAN" TO AN IMMORTAL.
AND TO THINK THAT SHE BETRAYED THE VERY ONES WHO GAVE HER DIVINE STATUS! A WENCH LIKE THAT COULD VERY WELL TURN ON US ANY MINUTE, TOO!
I WOULD EVEN GO SO FAR AS TO SAY THAT SHE'S THE KIND OF WOMAN THAT WOULD GET PREGNANT WITH ASHURA'S CHILD, AND THEN SHARE THE BED OF HIS ENEMY. IF YOU CATCH MY DRIFT...
I HEAR YOU LOUD AND CLEAR. I ALWAYS FOUND IT DOUBTFUL THAT THE YOUNG PRINCE, TENOU, WAS EVER TAISHAKUTEN'S CHILD!
NOW THEN, IF YOU'LL EXCUSE US, MY LORD. I LOOK FORWARD TO HEARING NEWS OF ASHURA'S DEMISE.
TENOU. WE'RE LEAVING.
FATHER!

WHEN WILL QUEEN KENDAPPA COME TO ZENMI CASTLE TO PLAY HER MUSIC AGAIN?
SHE'LL BE HERE ON THE NEXT FULL MOON, TENOU. NOW, JOIN YOUR MOTHER. THE ASSEMBLY IS OVER.
YES, BISHAM-ONTEN.

WELL, BISHAMONTEN, NOW THAT EVERYONE'S LEFT...
...I PRESUME THAT YOU'LL BE SENDING SPIES AFTER OUR FOUR GODS. CORRECT?

NATURALLY, YOUR HIGHNESS. AS THE HEAD OF THE FOUR GODS...
...IT IS MY JOB TO SECURE YOUR REIGN. AND THAT MEANS SNIPPING OFF BUDS OF DISLOYALTY BEFORE THEY BLOSSOM.
THAT'S THE BISHAMONTEN I KNOW.
ASHURA! RUN!!

ARE THOSE FIREFLIES? NO WAIT! THE LIGHT'S COMING FROM THE SWORD! IT'S THE... THE YAMA SWORD!
IT'S LORD YASHA FOR SURE!!
MORE OF TAISHAKUTEN'S SCUM, EH?! COME AND TASTE MY BLADE!!

DON'T WASTE YOUR TIME, LORD YASHA!
THE YAMA SWORD IS MEANT FOR MUCH MORE WORTHY OPPONENTS THAN A HANDFUL OF TAISHAKUTEN'S DOGS!
?
TWIN MOON LEAVES FLY!

NOW, LORD YASHA, IF YOU WOULD FOLLOW ME, PLEASE...
WHO ARE YOU?
UNBELIEVABLE...! IT'S...

...GANDARAHJA! THE FLYING CASTLE OF QUEEN KENDAPPA!!

OH HO HO HO HO HO! YOU ARE TOO MUCH!
LOOKS LIKE LORD YASHA HAS SET A NEW RECORD IN IDIOCY!
I've had enough of this.
?
NOT ONLY DO YOU DISOBEY TAISHAKUTEN BUT NOW YOU'RE ON THE RUN FROM HIM? YOU SURE KNOW HOW TO MAKE TROUBLE FOR YOURSELF!

IF YOU KNOW EVERYTHING THAT'S HAPPENED, WHY DID YOU LET US INTO YOUR CASTLE? YOU KNOW THE DANGERS, DON'T YOU?
"WHY," YOU ASK?
DON'T PULL THAT FEIGNED IGNORANCE WITH ME, BIG BROTHER! I WAS ONLY ACTING AS ANY LOVING SISTER WOULD!
Ha ha ha!
ER, I DON'T REMEMBER ANY YOUNGER SISTER. YOUNGER BROTHER, YES...BUT SISTER?
HOW COULD YOUR HEART HAVE GROWN SO COLD?!
YASHA, WHAT'S A MISTRESS?
I'll tell you when you're older.
WHO IS THIS CHILD?
DON'T TELL ME...YOU HAVE A MISTRESS NOW?!
WHAT KIND OF DIRTY BEHAVIOR IS THAT FOR A LORD?! IT'S FILTHY!
FILTHY!!
IT MUST BE THE FATE OF THOSE BORN TO A MISTRESS TO STRAY FROM THE RIGHT PATH LIKE THIS.

MY LADY, SUCH RUDE CONDUCT IS ENTIRELY UNCALLED FOR.
I'M SORRY. I KNEW THIS WOULD HAPPEN WHEN I SAW HIM.
QUEEN KENDAPPA...
IS IT... BECAUSE OF WHAT HAPPENED TO YOUR MOTHER?
EVEN THOUGH IT WAS A LONG TIME AGO, I CAN'T SO EASILY FORGET. MY MOTHER, THOUGH A MARRIED WOMAN...
...TOOK ONE LOOK AT LORD YASHA AND FELL CAPTIVE TO HIS CHARM RIGHT THEN AND THERE.
BUT SHE WAS BOUND BY HER MARRIAGE TO MY FATHER, AND SPENT EVERY DAY WEEPING FOR HER IMPOSSIBLE SITUATION, UNTIL FINALLY HER BROKEN HEART COULDN'T TAKE IT ANYMORE AND SHE DIED. I KNOW LORD YASHA DIDN'T DO ANYTHING WRONG...
...BUT I CAN'T HELP BUT HOLD A GRUDGE AGAINST HIM FOR HER DEATH. I KNOW I SHOULDN'T, BUT... STILL...

...I WON'T LIE
IT FELT GOOD
GIVING HIM
A GOOD
SWING WITH
MY HARP.
BUT,
SOUMA...
IF YOU
TELL ME TO
DO SO,
I'LL GLADLY
CORRECT MY
BEHAVIOR.
THANK
YOU...
...MY
LADY.

WOW, GETTING TO SLEEP UNDER A ROOF AGAIN...
I'D ALMOST FORGOTTEN WHAT IT FEELS LIKE!
HOW'S YOUR HEAD, YASHA? QUEEN KENDAPPA SURE IS STRONG, ISN'T SHE?
THAT'S THE FIRST TIME I'VE GOTTEN SUCH A BEATING!
GIGEI WAS STRONG TOO, WASN'T SHE?
NOT JUST HER BODY. HER SPIRIT WAS STRONG AS WELL.
I SURE MISS GIGEI...
MMM.
SHE'S PROBABLY ON HER WAY HERE RIGHT NOW. I CAN'T WAIT TO SEE HER...
I MUST THANK GIGEI WHEN I SEE HER AGAIN.
ME NEITHER, ASHURA...
IT'S BEEN A LONG TIME SINCE ASHURA'S SLEPT WITH SUCH A PEACEFUL FACE...

じーい
UH...WHAT DO YOU THINK YOU'RE DOING?
ころん
ぽてっ
ぱん ぱん
I CAME TO WAKE YOU UP.
YOU THINK I LET YOU INTO MY CASTLE JUST TO HANG OUT?
NO. SO TELL ME WHAT IT IS YOU WANT.

IF YOU'D STEP INSIDE, PLEASE...
K-KISSHOUTEN!
WHAT IS THIS...?
SHE INSISTED ON SEEING YOU, EVEN IF ONLY THROUGH THE STAR MIRROR.
IT'S BEEN A WHILE, LORD YASHA.
YOU'RE LOOKING A LITTLE RAGGED.
IT'S A ROUGH LIFE, I TAKE IT. FOR BOTH YOU AND THE ASHURA CHILD. YOU HAVE MY PITY.

YASHA...
WHERE'D YOU GO...?
Mmmm..
I NEED YOU TO TIE MY HAIR UP...
I HOPE GIGEI CAN STILL CATCH UP WITH US...
WOW, THIS CASTLE'S REALLY FLYING! AND SO HIGH UP, TOO...
AS BISHAMONTEN'S WIFE, I AM BOUND BY LOYALTY AND POWERLESS TO DO ANYTHING AGAINST TAISHAKUTEN'S ORDERS. BUT THE PAIN OF WITNESSING IN SILENCE ALL HIS ACTS OF EVIL...IF ONLY I COULD HAVE DONE SOMETHING.
POOR GIGEI...SO YOUNG AND TALENTED... AND WHEN SHE WAS KILLED BEFORE MY VERY EYES, I COULDN'T EVEN PICK UP THE BODY. I COULDN'T DO ANYTHING.

I CAN'T TAKE THIS ANY LONGER...I DON'T WANT TO SEE ANY MORE INNOCENTS DIE AT THAT MAN'S HANDS.
GIGEI WAS...
GIGEI WAS KILLED...?

PLEASE LET ME HELP YOU.
KISSHOUTEN!! THAT'S TOO DANGEROUS FOR SOMEONE IN YOUR POSITION!
......
I SHALL GIVE YOU SOUMA TO ACCOMPANY YOU.
YOU SAW HER SKILLS.
SHE'S THE LAST REMAINING MEMBER OF THE SOUMA TRIBE, ALCHEMISTS TO THE GOD KING.
SHE WISHES TO JOIN YOU AND AVENGE HER SLAUGHTERED TRIBE. GRANT HER THAT MUCH, AT LEAST.

THIS IS ALL I ASK FOR, LORD YASHA.
YOU DO REALIZE YOU MAY LOSE YOUR LIFE IF YOU JOIN US, DON'T YOU?
ALL TOO WELL.
SOUMA, YOU FOOL! YOU'RE ASKING FOR YOUR DEATH WISH!
DO YOU KNOW THE "SOUMA LEGEND"?

THE BLOOD OF A SOUMA CAN GRANT IMMORTALITY TO WHOMEVER DRINKS IT... THOUGH IT CAN ONLY BE DONE BUT ONCE IN THEIR LIFE.
THAT'S RIGHT.
TAISHAKUTEN WIPED OUT THE SOUMAS TO ENSURE THAT NO ONE WOULD DRINK THE LIFE-GIVING BLOOD...
HOWEVER, I ALONE ESCAPED AND FOUND REFUGE WITH QUEEN KENDAPPA.
AS TAISHAKUTEN'S LOYAL MUSICIAN, SHE THOUGHT IT TOO DANGEROUS FOR ME TO REMAIN HERE, SO SHE LEFT ME TO KISSHOUTEN.
ずか
ずか
OH! GOOD MORNING, QUEEN KENDAPPA!
わしゃ
WILL YOU TIE MY HAIR?
ムカ
FINE.
Ouch!

HEY, WHY WERE YOU ANGRY?
BECAUSE THE PERSON I LOVE IS LEAVING ON A JOURNEY. A JOURNEY SHE'LL PROBABLY NEVER RETURN FROM. I'M ANGRY AT HER FOR RISKING HER LIFE LIKE THAT...BUT I STILL LOVE HER.
AND I WAS JUST UPSET WITH MYSELF FOR BEING SO STUPID AS TO LOVE A FOOL LIKE HER.
RIGHT...I DON'T QUITE UNDERSTAND...
BUT I CAN TELL THIS MUCH. YOU'RE VERY STRONG FOR NOT CRYING ABOUT IT.
IF I COULDN'T SEE SOME-ONE I LOVED ANYMORE...
...I'D DEFINITELY CRY.

SOUMA'S STRONG, TOO.
Woosh!
Twin Moon Leaves Fly!
AND YASHA TOO. I LIKE STRONG PEOPLE BECAUSE EVEN IF THEY'RE WITH ME, THEY DON'T DIE.
OH, BY THE WAY! COULD YOU MAKE THE CASTLE MOVE SLOWER? A FRIEND'S SUPPOSED TO JOIN US, AND SHE WON'T BE ABLE TO FOLLOW US IF WE'RE MOVING SO FAST. HER NAME'S GIGEI.
WHAT..?
GIGEI...? DO YOU MEAN THE DANCER...
...WHO WAS KILLED BY THE GOD KING'S ARMY?
WHAT DO YOU MEAN...?

THEY SAID THAT I'M BAD LUCK AND THAT I BRING EVERYONE DEATH...
GIGEI!
THAT'S NOT TRUE AT ALL.
I'M HAPPY WHEN I'M WITH YOU. YOU MAKE ME HAPPY.
I LOVE YOU, ASHURA.
I LOVE YOU.
NO...NO, IT CAN'T BE...
SHE SAID... SHE PROMISED SHE'D COME FOR US...!!

ASHURA?
ASHURA?!
SOB...
SOB...
GIGEI...!

GIGEI...

I HAVEN'T TOLD HER YET THAT I LOVE HER, TOO.

I DIDN'T GET TO TELL HER.

GIGEI... WHY...?

OH NO. I'VE MADE HIM CRY.
IF SOUMA FINDS OUT, SHE'LL REALLY GET ON MY TAIL ABOUT IT.
......
WHO'S THERE?!
NAUGHTY, NAUGHTY BOY! DON'T YOU KNOW EAVESDROPPING IS RUDE?!

WHO SENT YOU?!
OUT WITH IT! WHAT, NOT GONNA TALK? AREN'T YOU A STUBBORN ONE!
Spies are always so tight-lipped...
Oof! Urgh!
I DON'T KNOW WHO YOU ARE...
Ghhrrgh! I'm gonna die! I'm gonna die!
...BUT I'M IN A PRETTY SOUR MOOD.
AND NOW I WANT TO TAKE IT OUT ON SOMEONE.

ASHURA.
WHERE HAVE YOU BEEN?
HOW MANY TIMES HAVE I TOLD YOU NOT TO WANDER OFF ALONE?
WE NEVER KNOW WHERE THE GOD KING'S ARMY MAY BE WAITING FOR US. EVEN IN THIS VERY CASTLE!

ARE YOU LISTENING TO ME, ASHURA?!
Sniffle... sob...
WHAT HAPPENED?

YASHA, DID YOU KNOW...
...THAT... GIGEI...
...WAS KILLED?

DID YOU?!

I'M STILL WAITING FOR YOUR BOSS' NAME.
YOU DO REALIZE THAT IN TRESPASSING INTO MY CASTLE...
...I HAVE THE RIGHT TO SPEAK WITH YOUR SUPERIOR ABOUT YOUR MISBEHAVIOR.
UGH...!
UGGGH...!
HM, YOU LOOK OLD ENOUGH TO HAVE A WIFE AND CHILDREN. BUT HERE YOU ARE, A FACELESS CRONY FOR SOME LOWLIFE CREEP.
JUST WHAT WAS IT YOU WERE LOOKING FOR HERE?
YOU'D BETTER MAKE YOUR ANSWER FAST.
YOU DON'T HAVE THAT MUCH TIME.

UGGGGGH...!
BINGO.
WELL! THAT DIDN'T TAKE LONG AT ALL. I THOUGHT YOU'D BE MORE OF A MATCH...
THIS CREST...IT'S THE INSIGNIA OF BISHAMONTEN'S ARMY.
CHOKING HIM LIKE THAT...
...HE COULDN'T HAVE SAID ANYTHING EVEN IF HE WANTED TO, QUEEN KENDAPPA.

SOUMA!
QUEEN KENDAPPA... I WISH YOU'D HAVE LEFT SUCH DIRTY BUSINESS TO ME.
AFTER ALL, YOU ARE THE ROYAL MUSICIAN.
IT'S A SHAME TO HAVE YOUR BEAUTIFUL HANDS STAINED WITH BLOOD LIKE THIS...

SOUMA, I'M GOING TO BE FRANK WITH YOU. IF YOU GO WITH LORD YASHA TOMORROW, I'M AFRAID YOU'LL END UP LIKE THIS MAN HERE.

DO YOU DOUBT MY SKILLS?
NO, IT'S NOT THAT. BUT...
IT'S JUST... TAISHAKUTEN'S ALREADY SENDING SPIES TO MY CASTLE. DO YOU STILL HAVE TO LEAVE?
I'M SORRY...I CAN'T TELL YOU WHAT TO DO. IF YOU MUST GO... I'LL UNDERSTAND.
BUT PLEASE PROMISE ME ONE THING.
DON'T GET YOURSELF KILLED AND LEAVE ME ALONE.
I SEE...
THEN KEEP THIS FOR ME UNTIL I RETURN.
I PROMISE TO FINISH MY JOB AND COME BACK TO YOU, MY LADY...

......
I WON'T..
...SEE YOU OFF.
THERE'S NO POINT IN SAYING GOODBYE IF YOU'LL BE COMING RIGHT BACK, RIGHT?
YOU PROMISED YOU'D RETURN, SO...
...UNTIL THEN, I WON'T GIVE THIS BACK TO YOU.
I PROMISE...
...MY KENDAPPA.

IT WAS BECAUSE SHE WAS WITH ME...!
IT'S BECAUSE OF ME...
...THAT GIGEI HAD TO DIE!
EVERYONE WHO COMES NEAR ME DIES.
YOU, TOO. IF YOU STAY WITH ME, YOU'LL DIE SOMEDAY, TOO.
ALL BECAUSE OF ME.
BUT I DON'T WANT YOU TO DIE, YASHA... DON'T DIE BECAUSE OF ME!

ASHURA, DO YOU THINK I'M THAT WEAK? I'M THE BEST GUARDIAN WARRIOR IN TENKAI!
YOU DON'T THINK SUCH A PERSON CAN BE KILLED, DO YOU?

ぶん
ぶん

THEN I'M STAYING BY YOUR SIDE. TOGETHER, WE'LL DEFEAT TAISHAKUTEN AND MAKE TENKAI A BETTER PLACE.
NO ONE WILL BE HUNTED ANYMORE. NO ONE WILL DIE ANYMORE.

UNTIL THEN, WE'LL STAY TOGETHER.
I'LL NEVER LEAVE YOU, ASHURA. I'M HERE TO PROTECT YOU.

PROMISE ME! PROMISE ME, GOT IT?!
Cross your heart and hope to die!

PATERNAL INSTINCTS KICKING IN, EH, LORD YASHA?
KUJAKU...
THANKS FOR THE MEAL THE OTHER DAY.
Pardon my intrusion...
HOW DID YOU GET INSIDE?
THIS CASTLE'S PROTECTED BY A SHIELD AGAINST YOUR KIND.
THANKS TO MY BODY, SHIELDS DON'T WORK AGAINST ME. I'VE GOT FREE ACCESS TO ANYWHERE.
OHO!
SO THE LITTLE DEVIL'S ASLEEP, EH?

THAT'S TOO BAD...I WAS HOPING I COULD PLAY WITH HIM A BIT.
HUH...OUT LIKE A LIGHT. I WONDER... MAYBE IF I PINCHED HIM...
DON'T EVEN TRY IT.
Tee hee!
UH-OH! DADDY'S MAD!
OUT WITH IT. WHAT ARE YOU DOING HERE? WHY DO YOU KEEP BOTHERING US?
I'M JUST WORRIED ABOUT ASHURA.
I CAME HERE TO WARN YOU TWO FOR THE LITTLE DARLING'S SAKE.
THERE'S ANOTHER INTRUDER HERE BESIDES ME. A RAT SENT BY THE GOD KING.
A SPY FROM BISHAMONTEN'S ARMY?
BINGO!
Yeah!
どんどん!♪

OH...AND ONE MORE THING.
I HAVE A BIT OF INFORMATION FOR YOU.
IF YOU WANT TO FIND THE SIX STARS, YOU MUST FIND THE SHURA SWORD FIRST.
THE SHURA SWORD?!

IT IS THE LEGENDARY SWORD FROM THE DAWN OF TENKAI'S CREATION. A SWORD THAT ONLY THE KING OF THE ASHURA MAY WIELD.
ONE SWING VANQUISHES ALL EVIL WITH ITS MIGHTY BLAZE.
AS LONG AS THE SHURA SWORD EXISTS, TENKAI STILL HAS A CHANCE AT PEACE. ONCE REVIVED, THE TABLES WILL TURN AND TAISHAKUTEN WILL BE NO MORE.

IF ASHURA REVIVES THE SHURA SWORD, HE CAN USE IT TO LOCATE THE SIX STARS.
HOW DO YOU KNOW ALL THIS?

JUST WHAT ARE YOU AFTER?

MORE IMPORTANTLY, WHO ARE YOU, KUJAKU? ARE YOU ONE OF THE SIX STARS?

I APPRECIATE YOUR WARNING...

BUT THOUGH YOU SAY YOU'RE NOT MY ENEMY...YOU'RE NOT ONE OF THE SIX STARS EITHER. AND I DON'T LIKE HAVING A SKETCHY GUY LIKE YOU HANGING AROUND ALL THE TIME.
NO NEED TO JUMP THE SWORD. IT'S NOT LIKE I'M ONE OF TAISHAKUTEN'S GOONS.

SORRY! CLOSE, BUT NO CIGAR!
Oops!

THEY SAY THE SHURA SWORD LIES IN THE BORDERLANDS TO THE WEST. IT'S SEALED DEEP WITHIN KUSUMAPURA... THE UNDERGROUND CASTLE OF KUMARATEN, KING OF THE UNDERWORLD.

THANKS FOR YOUR HELP. I WON'T TELL QUEEN KENDAPPA ABOUT YOU. I OWE YOU THAT MUCH.
Bye-bye.
NOW GET OUTTA HERE.

WHAT'S IT TO YOU IF WE RETRIEVE THE SHURA SWORD AND FIND ALL THE SIX STARS? WHY ARE YOU SO INTERESTED?
IT'S ENTERTAINING FOR ME. DON'T WORRY, I WISH YOU THE BEST OF LUCK IS ALL.

YOU'RE A FAIR GUY. I'LL GIVE YOU THAT.

SOUMA, YOU SURE YOU'RE OKAY WITH LEAVING WITHOUT SAYING YOUR FAREWELLS TO QUEEN KENDAPPA LIKE THIS?
YES. I KNOW THIS WAY IS BEST.
IT'S MY DUTY TO PROTECT YOU FROM WHATEVER LURKS IN THE SHADOWS.
THE GOD KING'S ARMY IS NEAR. ALLOW ME TO GO AND INVESTIGATE THEIR ACTIVITY.
EXCUSE ME.

IS THAT CRYING? NO...IT'S A HARP...

QUEEN KENDAPPA. PLEASE DON'T PLAY SO SADLY.
YASHA...

YOU'RE AWAKE, ASHURA?
YASHA...
WHAT'S THAT MUSIC?
IT SOUNDS SO SAD.
THE ONE WHO LEFT FOR A JOURNEY...THE ONE QUEEN KENDAPPA LOVES...AND EVERYONE...
I HOPE NONE OF THEM DIE. I DON'T WANT ANYONE ELSE TO DIE...

FIRST THE PEOPLE OF THE YASHA VILLAGE... THEN GIGEI...

I DON'T WANT PEOPLE AROUND ME TO DIE ANYMORE.

IF ONLY I WERE STRONGER...IF I HAD BEEN STRONG ENOUGH TO DEFEAT TAISHAKUTEN, MAYBE GIGEI WOULDN'T HAVE HAD TO DIE.

I DON'T WANT TO LOSE SOMEONE LIKE GIGEI AGAIN.
EVER AGAIN.
I WANT TO BE STRONG.
TO PROTECT THOSE I LOVE...

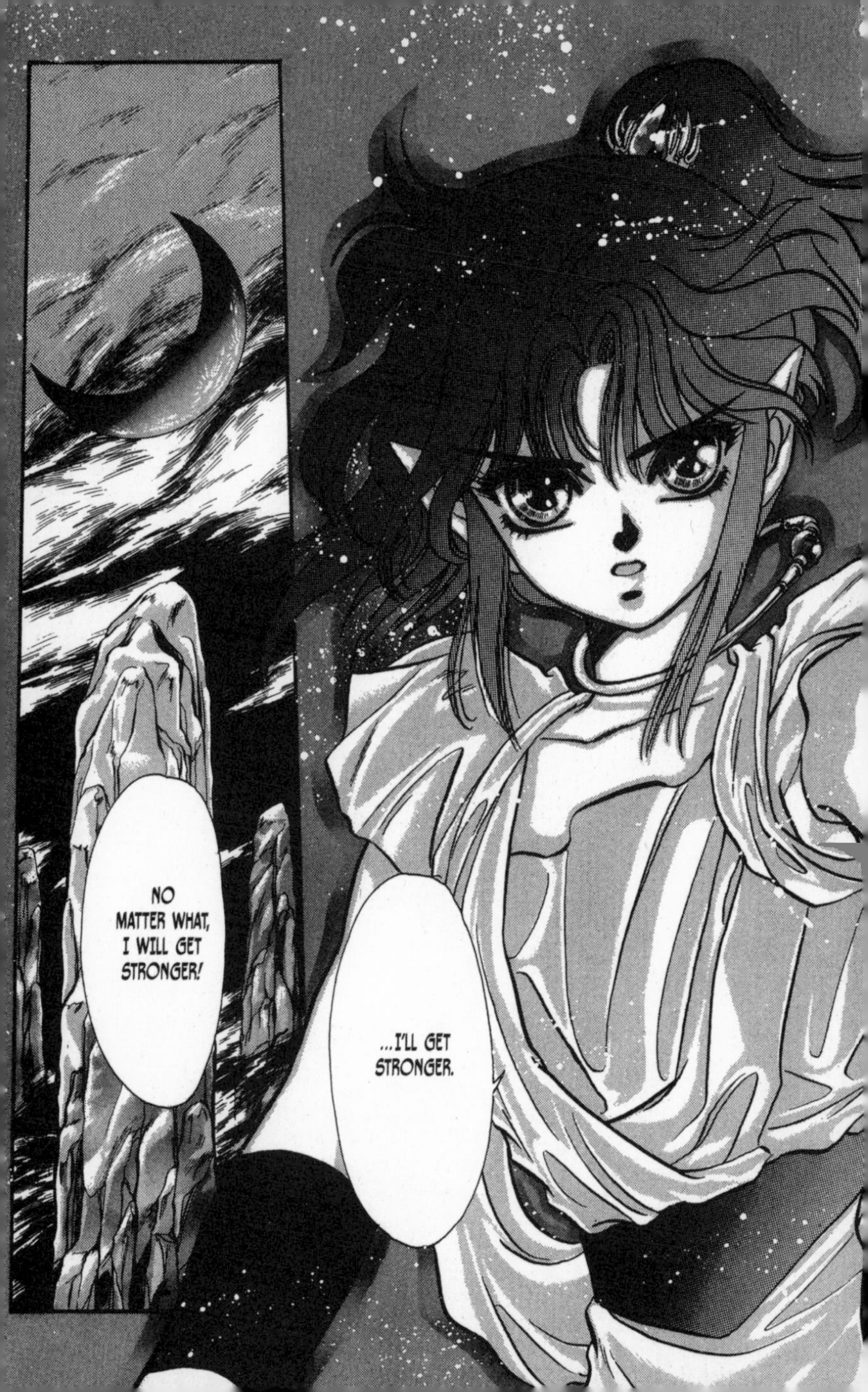
...I'LL GET STRONGER.
NO MATTER WHAT, I WILL GET STRONGER!

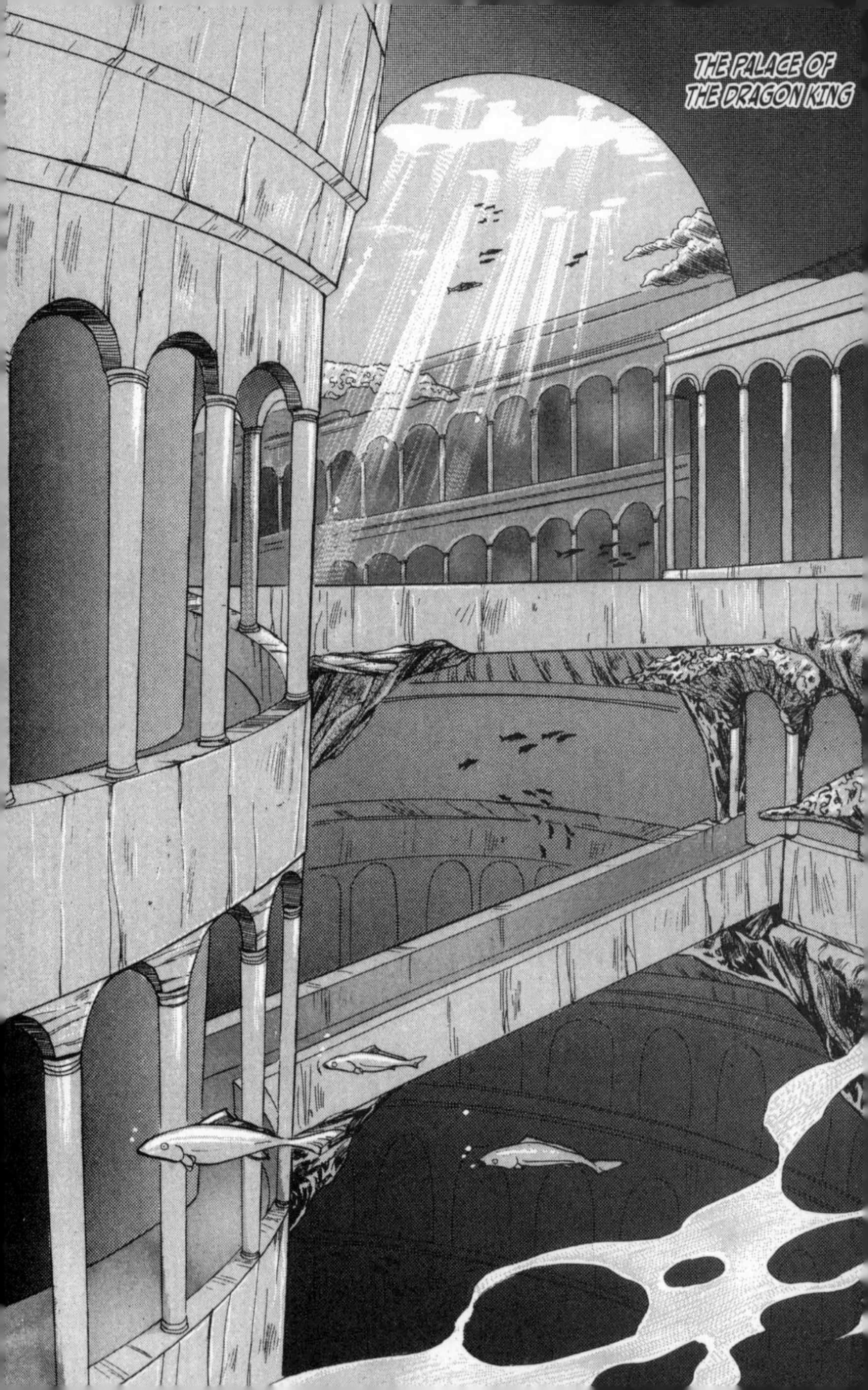
THE PALACE OF
THE DRAGON KING

NO WAY!
WHY DO I HAVE TO WEAR THIS STUPID THING?!
KYAAAA
NAHGA!! YOU KNOW THAT EVERY KING MUST WEAR THAT GARB!
KYAAAA
YOU CAN'T MAKE ME BE THE DRAGON KING!!

NAHGA, STOP MAKING A FUSS.
HAKURYUU! SEIRYUU!!*
NAHGA...
NAHGA, YOUR GRANDFATHER IS ILL.
AND YOU KNOW VERY WELL THAT YOU'RE THE ONLY GRANDCHILD HE HAS. WHO ELSE CAN BE THE SUCCESSOR BUT YOU?
PHOOIE!
SOMEONE WHO WANTS TO BECOME THE DRAGON KING SHOULD SUCCEED!!

*HAKURYUU MEANS "WHITE DRAGON" AND SEIRYUU MEANS "BLUE DRAGON."

DON'T BE RIDICULOUS! THE BLOODLINE MUST CONTINUE!
SAY WHATEVER YOU WANT...THE INAUGURATION CEREMONY IS IN TEN DAYS AND THERE'S NOTHING YOU CAN DO ABOUT IT!

JUST TRY IT! I'M NOT GONNA BECOME THE DRAGON KING! I'M NOT!!

You little...!! You can't win!

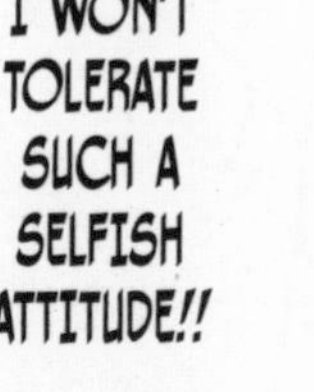
I WON'T TOLERATE SUCH A SELFISH ATTITUDE!!

OH, BOY...
Someone's gonna pop a vein...
SOB
HE HATES THE IDEA THAT MUCH...?

I WON'T LET YOU TIE ME DOWN TO THE THRONE LIKE THAT!
I'LL LEAD MY LIFE THE WAY I WANT TO!
NAHGA!!!

NAHGA!!
KYAA!
MASTER NAHGA!

HAKURYUU... DO SOME-THING...
I KNOW, SIRE.
SOB SOB
おうおう

SEIRYUU!!
?

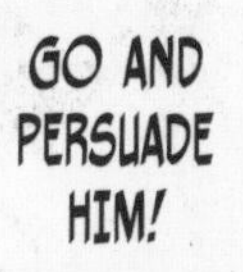
GO AND PERSUADE HIM!

Great.
THIS AIN'T GONNA BE PRETTY...
BIG BRO AND NAHGA ARE SO DARN STUBBORN. WHY DO THEY HAVE TO MAKE THINGS DIFFICULT...
NAHGA?

NAHGA...
IT'S BEEN A WHILE...
...SINCE EITHER OF YOU HAVE TAKEN ME ON AS A RIVAL IN SWORDSMANSHIP.
WHAT?
What's that have to do with anything?
WHOA!
IS IT BECAUSE I'M THE SUCCESSOR TO THE DRAGON KING?
IS THAT WHY YOU WON'T PRACTICE WITH ME ANYMORE?! HUH?!

OH.
AH HA HA HA HA HA HA HA!
WHAT?!
IDIOT.
OF COURSE THAT'S NOT WHY.
LISTEN, NAHGA.
WE DON'T PRACTICE WITH YOU...
...BECAUSE WE DON'T NEED TO ANYMORE. YOU'VE GOTTEN STRONGER, AND NOW YOU'RE STRONG ENOUGH TO BE THE KING OF DRAGON TRIBE, THE GUARDIAN WARRIORS OF THE WESTLAND. YOU'RE WAY OUT OF OUR LEAGUE NOW.

NOW DO YOU UNDERSTAND? THEN GO APOLOGIZE TO HAKURYUU.
TELL HIM THAT YOU ACCEPT YOUR DUTY AS THE DRAGON KING. I KNOW YOU'LL MAKE A GOOD KING.
What's that supposed to mean?
IN FACT, BOTH HAKURYUU AND I ARE LOOKING FORWARD TO YOUR BECOMING KING.
SEIRYUU...
とん…

JEEZ, I CAN'T TAKE THIS!
WHY DOES MY FUTURE HAVE TO BE DECIDED SO EARLY LIKE THIS?!
ボウ
HUH?
WHAT'S THIS? INTRUDERS AT THE EAST SHIELD?
THAT'S THE FAMED LORD YASHA.
WHAT'S HE DOING HERE?
THIS COULD BE INTERESTING...
Hee hee hee.

AH HA HA HA HA!
I COULDN'T HAVE ASKED FOR A MORE WORTHY OPPONENT!

I MAY JUST...
...GET TO HAVE A BOUT WITH THE BEST GUARDIAN WARRIOR IN TENKAI!!
SUPER LUCKY!
PEACE!

YASHA! LOOK! LOOK! THE WATER'S SO BEAUTIFUL, AND FULL OF FISH, TOO! ♡
THIS IS THE WEST END OF TENKAI. THE LAND OF THE DRAGON TRIBE, GUARDIANS OF WATER.
THE RICHEST WATERS IN TENKAI ARE HERE.
WOW...

!
WELL, WELL, WELL. IF IT ISN'T LORD YASHA...
FANCY FINDING YOU HERE!

I AM NAHGA,
GRANDSON OF
THE DRAGON KING,
AND SOON TO BE
GUARDIAN WARRIOR
OF THE WESTLAND.

H-HEY!
WHERE DO YOU THINK YOU'RE GOING?!
......
FOR TRESPASSING ON OUR LANDS, I CHALLENGE YOU TO A MATCH!

DIDN'T YOU HEAR ME?!
HOW DARE YOU IGNORE ME!
LOOKS LIKE THE RUMORS ARE TRUE. YOU'VE GOT SOME ATTITUDE.
Jerk.
じぃーーっ
WHAT'RE YOU LOOKING AT, KID?
HE OURS, ORD ASHA?

NO, I'M NOT!
OH REALLY?
ANYWAY, WHAT'RE YOU DOING HANGING AROUND HERE?
AIN'T THIS A LITTLE FAR FROM YOUR USUAL TERRITORY?
NOT AGAIN!
スタスタ!
HOLD IT RIGHT THERE!

YOU DEAF OR CHICKEN?
I CHALLENGED YOU TO A MATCH. I'M NOT GONNA LET YOU RUN AWAY FROM THAT.
YOU ARE *THE* LORD YASHA, AREN'T YOU?
I WANT TO SEE WHAT THE GREATEST GUARDIAN WARRIOR OF TENKAI HAS TO OFFER...

...AND
SHOW MY
SKILL IN
TURN!
COME ON!
DON'T TELL
ME IT'LL BE
THIS EASY!

くる くる
くる
WHOA!!
UGHF!
JUST WHAT I WAS EXPECTING! HE'S A STRONG OPPONENT!
NO MORE GAMES!
NOW I'M SERIOUS!
ばしゃ

HAAAA! TAKE THIS!
WATER DRAGONS GO!!!
NEPTUNE FORMATION STRIKE!!!

AND NOW...!
...EAT THIS!!

WHOA!
ERGH!
DAMMIT... MAYBE HE'S A LITTLE MORE THAN I CAN HANDLE...
YASHA.

I'M HUNGRY...
LET'S EAT.
WAY TO KILL THE MOOD

HELP YOURSELF TO THE VEGETABLES, TOO.
はぐはぐ
あぐあぐ
YOU KNOW, YOU INTERRUPTED A PERFECTLY GOOD MATCH WITH THAT DARN STOMACH OF YOURS.
There's more of it on your face than in your mouth.
SO... YOU'RE "ASHURA," EH?
THE ASHURAS ARE SUPPOSED TO BE AN INTELLIGENT, GOOD-LOOKING, ELEGANT RACE. HOW CAN AN UNRULY SHRIMP LIKE *YOU* BE ONE OF *THEM*?
Nurture over nature, I guess...
There's not a shred of refinement that I can see.
BESIDES, I THOUGHT THE ASHURAS WERE WIPED OUT AGES AGO...
JUST HOW OLD ARE YOU, KID?
UMM...THIS MANY.
3?
300.
YEAH, RIGHT.
UNBELIEVABLE...
ごろん!!
THEY ALWAYS SAY IT WAS A GOOD ERA, WITH LORD ASHURA LEADING THE FOUR GODS.
THE GODS WERE FRIENDS WHO *COOPERATED* TO GUARD THE NORTH, SOUTH, EAST AND WEST OF TENKAI. NOTHING LIKE THE SNOBBY FOUR GODS OF TODAY.

WHEN I BECOME DRAGON KING, I'LL BE WORKING UNDER KOUMOKUTEN, ONE OF THE FOUR GODS.
BUT NO MATTER WHAT THE OTHERS SAY, I CAN'T SEE HIM AS SOMEONE WORTH RISKING THE LIVES OF MY TRIBE.
YOU'RE GOING TO BECOME "DRAGON KING"?
YEAH, MY GRANDPA'S SICK, SO THAT PUTS ME NEXT IN LINE.
BUT...I DON'T WANT TO BE DRAGON KING.
ARE YOU...
...STRONG?
UH...YEAH, I GUESS.
AT LEAST, THAT'S WHAT SEIRYUU AND HAKURYUU SAY.
THEN YOU SHOULD BE FINE!
?
FINE? HOW?

YOU WON'T DIE BECAUSE OF ME.
YOU'LL BE ALL RIGHT...NO MATTER WHAT.

COME ON.
WE'RE GOING, ASHURA.
?
?
WAIT JUST A MINUTE HERE!
WHAT ABOUT OUR MATCH?!
I HAVE SOMEWHERE TO BE.

THEN I'M COMING WITH YOU!

YOU'RE THE SUCCESSOR TO THE THRONE. YOU CAN'T JUST--

DIDN'T YOU HEAR WHAT I SAID?!
YOU AND I HAVE A SCORE TO SETTLE! AND UNTIL THEN...
...I'M NOT LETTING YOU GO SO EASILY!
WE'RE CONSIDERED TRAITORS BY THE GOD KING'S ARMY.
YOU DON'T WANT TO GET YOURSELF INVOLVED.
GET IT THROUGH YOUR HEAD. WE'RE OUT TO BRING DOWN TAISHAKUTEN.
SOUNDS LIKE FUN TO ME.
COUNT ME IN.
YASHA, LET NAHGA COME WITH US.
I WANT 'IM TO!

ぱんっ
BUT ASHURA... YOU USUALLY SAY YOU DON'T WANT PEOPLE TO COME WITH YOU...
ALL RIGHT THEN!
IF I'LL BE JOINING YOU, I HAVE A FEW THINGS TO SETTLE FIRST!
NAHGA?!
IF I'M GONNA BE GOING UP AGAINST THE GOD KING...
...I'M GONNA NEED A WEAPON, RIGHT?
AND LET'S JUST SAY I HAVE A LITTLE BUSINESS TO TAKE CARE OF...
MASTER HAKURYUU!
MASTER SEIRYUU!
LORD NAHGA HAS RETURNED!

NAHGA!!
だかだかだかだか
WHERE THE HELL HAVE YOU BEEN?!
YOU'VE HAD US LOOKING EVERYWHERE FOR YOU!!
I'VE DECIDED... TO FULFILL THE ROLE OF DRAGON KING.
YOU'RE... YOU'RE SERIOUS?
ふるふるふるふる
YEAH, I SAID I'LL BECOME THE DRAGON KING.
WHAT? NOW YOU HAVE A PROBLEM WITH THAT?
THIS IS FANTASTIC!
がばっ
I KNEW YOU'D COME TO YOUR SENSES SOON ENOUGH!
GAH!
WE HAVE TO PREPARE FOR THE CEREMONY! HURRY!!

THIS IS THE SUBTERRAIN OF THE DRAGON PALACE.
THE DEPTHS OF THESE WATERS HOLD A VERY PRECIOUS SWOR--
YEAH, YEAH. ALL I GOTTA DO IS PULL THE SWORD OUT FROM THE BOTTOM, RIGHT? PIECE OF CAKE.
GUESS THE TRICK IS BEING *WORTHY* OF BECOMING THE NEXT KING. IF THE SWORD DOESN'T RECOGNIZE ME AS KING, IT WON'T BUDGE.

HOW FAR DOWN DOES THIS THING GO?
THE "DRAGON FANG SWORD"... LEGEND HAS IT THAT IT'S THE KEY TO OPENING THE GATE AT THE BOTTOM OF THIS LAKE, THE GATE THAT HOLDS ALL THE EVILS OF THE WATER WORLD SEALED WITHIN.
PULLING OUT THE DRAGON FANG SWORD AND RESEALING THE EVILS IS ALL PART OF THE CEREMONY OF BECOMING KING.
THERE IT IS!!

AND THIS MUST BE... THE GATE.
THE DRAGON FANG SWORD...
THE TOKEN OF THE DRAGON KING.
ぎゅっ
IF I PULL THIS OUT, I'LL BECOME THE DRAGON KING, RULER OF THE WATER WORLD...

WE'RE OUT TO BRING DOWN TAISHAKUTEN.
I KNOW YOU'LL MAKE A GOOD KING.
ARE YOU...
...STRONG?
I CAN DO THIS.
ゴボ

オオ
ズ!!ズズズズズズ…
STRONGER! STRONGER THAN EVER BEFORE!
I'LL BE... I'LL BE STRONG!

ゴオオォオ

I DID IT...I DID IT!!
FINALLY...
...THE DRAGON FANG SWORD...
WITH THIS, I'LL BE READY FOR ANY MATCH!!
YOU HEAR ME, LORD YASHA?!

GASP!

IS THAT HIM? IS HE BACK?

HAKURYUU!

NOT SO FAST, YOU!

WHERE DO YOU THINK YOU'RE GOING, NAHGA?!
HAKURYUU ?!

THERE ARE SO MANY PEOPLE STRONGER THAN ME IN TENKAI.
SO FOR THE SAKE OF THE TRIBE, I NEED TO GET STRONGER!
I'LL COME BACK WHEN I'M STRONG ENOUGH TO LOOK AFTER THE DRAGON TRIBE.
Wha ?!
UNTIL THEN, KEEP GRANDPA ALIVE, OKAY?
NAHGA.
NOW THAT YOU HAVE THE DRAGON FANG SWORD...
...YOU *ARE* THE KING OF THE DRAGONS.
AND ALL I CAN DO IS OBEY MY KING'S ORDERS.
HAKURYUU...

OOF!
WHAT WAS THAT FOR?!
FAREWELL.
I SHALL SUPPORT YOU IN WHATEVER DECISION YOU MAKE...
...MY LORD.
WAIT JUST A LITTLE LONGER, YASHA!
SEE?!
Phew!
THERE HE IS! I KNEW HE'D COME BACK!

FROM NOW ON...
...YOU CAN CALL ME "LORD RYUU."
LORD RYUU?
YEAH, LORD RYUU, THE DRAGON KING.
HOW ABOUT "RYUUY" FROM NOW ON?
WHAT?! NO!
RYUUY! I'M HUNGRY!
RETURN TO YOUR PALACE, LORD RYUU.
YOU'RE JEOPARDIZING THE SAFETY OF THE DRAGON TRIBE.
WHEN TAISHAKUTEN FINDS OUT THAT YOU'RE INVOLVED WITH US, HE WILL CONSIDER YOU AND YOUR KIND TRAITORS.

IN THIS WORLD OF THE GOD KING, A SINGLE REBEL CAN SPELL OUT THE DEMISE OF HIS ENTIRE RACE.
BE A RESPONSIBLE KING. THINK OF YOUR TRIBE'S SAFETY.
I'M TELLING YOU, LORD RYUU... GO BACK TO YOUR PEOPLE.
REBEL?!
AH HA HA HA HA
Hee hee hee.
I'M NO REBEL! I'M JUST ON A TRIP TO PERFECT MY SKILL!
THIS IS JUST FOR ME! TAISHAKUTEN CAN'T PIN ME FOR TREACHERY SO HE CAN'T HURT ME OR MY PEOPLE.
YASHA, LET HIM COME WITH US!
DO AS YOU WISH.
わーい
IF YOU WANT TO FIND THE SIX STARS, YOU MUST FIND THE SHURA SWORD FIRST.
THEY SAY THE SHURA SWORD LIES IN THE BORDERLANDS TO THE WEST. IT'S SEALED DEEP WITHIN "KUSUMAPURA", THE UNDERGROUND CASTLE OF KUMARATEN, KING OF THE UNDERWORLD.

KUJAKU... IT'S NOT THAT I BELIEVE EVERYTHING YOU SAY...
...BUT I WOULD GO TO THE ENDS OF THE WORLD...
...TO FIND FIND THE SHURA SWORD... FIND THE SIX STARS...
...AND BRING DOWN TAISHAKUTEN.

THAT'S RIGHT... JUST A LITTLE CLOSER...
...CHILD OF THE ASHURA.

KUSUMAPURA WILL BE YOUR GRAVEYARD.

I INTEND TO DESTROY TAISHAKUTEN WITH THE "SHURA SWORD," AND THAT MEANS AN ASHURA SACRIFICE.

WHERE ARE WE GOING, LORD YASHA?!
TAISHAKUTEN IS IN THE OPPOSITE DIRECTION! SO WHY ARE WE HEADING TO THE FOREST?

WE'RE GOING TO KUSUMAPURA.

WHAT?! WHY?! THAT PLACE IS NOTHING MORE THAN RUINS!

I'M HUNGRY, RYUUY.

YOU JUST ATE TWO MINUTES AGO!!

わーわーっ
Why you!!
Nya ha ha ha.
...SOUMA.
YOU'RE TOO KEEN, LORD YASHA.
WHO ARE YOU?!
MY NAME IS SOUMA.
AND YOU'RE THE DRAGON KING, CORRECT?

? ?
HOW DID YOU KNOW THAT I BECAME THE DRAGON KING?
I LEFT AS SOON AS THE CEREMONY FINISHED, AND I HAVEN'T SEEN ANYONE ELSE SINCE THEN, SO--
MY JOB IS TO ASSIST LORD YASHA...
...AND PROTECT THE HOLY CHILD OF THE ASHURA.
NATURALLY I KNOW EVERYTHING ABOUT YOU.
H holy child?

YOU SAYING THAT THIS LITTLE PIGGY'S A HOLY CHILD?
DON'T CALL ME THAT!

WHY NOT? EVERY TIME YOU OPEN YOUR MOUTH, IT'S "I'M HUNGRY!" "FEED ME!"
THINGS HAVE GOTTEN LOUDER SINCE I'VE LEFT.

I WARNED HIM ABOUT JOINING US, BUT HE WOULDN'T LISTEN...
THE GOD KING'S PUNISHMENT FOR MUTINY IS "DEATH." I CAN ONLY HOPE HIS TRIBE WON'T BE HELD SUSPECT BECAUSE THEIR KING HAS JOINED US...

WHAT'S THERE TO LAUGH ABOUT?

YOU NEVER HEARD THE RUMORS? YOU'RE THE "FIERCEST GUARDIAN WARRIOR IN TENKAI. EVEN EVIL COWERS AT THE VERY SOUND OF YOUR NAME!"
BUT YOU'RE NOTHING LIKE THAT...
It's a welcome surprise.
SOUMA.
DO YOU KNOW OF "KUSUMAPURA" AT THE BORDERS OF THE WESTLANDS?
He's never heard the rumors.
He's not quite sure how to respond.
So he's changing the subject.
He's all flustered.

I'D HAVE NEVER DREAMED LORD YASHA COULD BE SO CONCERNED FOR OTHERS.

YES. WHERE KUMARATEN, KING OF THE UNDERWORLD IS SAID TO LIVE.
KUMARATEN'S RULE WAS ONE OF PROSPERITY AND FORTUNE.
WITH THE RICHES SUPPLIED BY UNDERGROUND RESOURCES, THE POPULATION THRIVED...
...AND THE FLOURISHING KUSUMAPURA WAS BESTOWED THE NAME, "THE FLOWER CAPITAL."
HOWEVER, DURING THE "HOLY WAR" 300 YEARS AGO, THE CASTLE AT THE BED OF THE EVERLASTING SPRING WAS DESTROYED.
THE ENTIRE TRIBE WAS EXTERMINATED AND THE CASTLE FELL INTO RUIN...
I HEAR THE SHURA SWORD IS IN KUSUMAPURA AND WE'RE OUT TO GET IT.
THE SHURA SWORD?! WHO TOLD YOU THAT?!

KUJAKU.
KUJAKU?
CAN WE REALLY BELIEVE WHAT HE SAYS?
THE SHURA SWORD IS THE KEY TO FINDING THE SIX STARS THAT WILL EVENTUALLY LEAD TO TAISHAKUTEN'S DESTRUCTION.
WE HAVE NO OTHER LEADS... SO I'M PUTTING MY FAITH IN HIS WORD.
YASHA, RYUUY IS PICKING ON ME!
I DON'T KNOW...BUT I HAVE NO CHOICE.
I SEE.

IN THAT CASE, IF YOU HEAD THIS WAY, YOU SHOULD COME ACROSS THE ENTRANCE INTO KUSUMAPURA THAT GOES THROUGH THE MOUNTAIN.

WHILE YOU GO DOWN TO THE UNDERGROUND CASTLE...
...I'LL ACT AS SENTRY OUTSIDE.

GOOD LUCK.
ASHURA, LORD RYUU...
TAKE CARE.
ハタ
ハタ!!
LOOK, THE INSIGNIA OF THE GOD'S ARMY.
YOU DON'T EVEN HAVE TO GUESS WHO'S HOLDING THE REINS AROUND HERE.

THIS IS IT. LET'S GO.
HEY, WAIT UP!

HEH. WELCOME TO KUSUMAPURA, LORD YASHA.
AND MY MOST PRECIOUS CHILD OF ASHURA...
WELL, KAHRA? DOES THIS SATISFY YOU?
IT'S A KEEPSAKE OF YOUR FORMER MASTER.

FOOLISH BRAT. HE'S WALKING RIGHT INTO HIS OWN GRAVE.
HE'S STILL YOUNG, BUT WITH THE FORMER KING DEAD, THAT MAKES HIM LORD ASHURA NOW.
KUMARATEN...
...DO YOU INTEND TO FIGHT THIS LORD ASHURA?
WHAT SORT OF CHALLENGE IS A *CHILD*?!

LET'S GO, OLD ONE.
WHERE TO, SIRE?
HE MAY BE YOUNG, BUT HE IS THE KING OF THE ASHURA.
SHOULDN'T WE GIVE HIM A PROPER WELCOME?

AS YOU WISH.
....

THIS IS IT?
THIS IS KUSUMAPURA, THE FLOWER CAPITAL?
IT'S NOTHING MORE THAN A GHOST TOWN NOW.
DOESN'T LOOK LIKE THERE'S A SOUL ALIVE...

HELLOOO!
WHAT ARE WE LOOKING FOR ANYWAY, LORD YASHA?
A SWORD.
IT SHOULD BE AT THE LOWEST LEVEL OF THE CASTLE.

THE SHURA SWORD.
KUJAKU SAID THE SHURA SWORD WOULD BE DEEP WITHIN KUSUMAPURA.
IF HE WAS TELLING THE TRUTH, THEN IT SHOULDN'T BE FAR NOW.
ガタガタ
ケホケホッ
ガラガラガラ
AH!
I JUST HOPE WE GET OUTTA THIS PLACE ALIVE!
カラン

WH-WHAT'S HAPPENING?!
THE FLOOR, IT'S...!
I'M SINKING!!
HELP ME!

YASHAAAA!!
ASHURA?!
DID YOU HEAR SOME-THING?
HEY!
ASHURA!!
YASHA!!

WHAT'S GOING ON?!
Ugh!
I'M COMING!
YASHA!! LOOK OUT!!

URGH!

YASHA!!
ASHURA!!

ASHURA!! NO!!
YA... SHA...
NO!!
WE'VE MADE IT THIS FAR...NOT NOW...!

ASHURAAAAA!!
Eek!
IS THIS...THE GOD KING ARMY'S DOING?

LORD YASHA! YOU'RE BLEEDING...!
I WAS CARELESS.
THIS ISN'T THE LOWEST LEVEL OF KUSUMAPURA. THERE MUST BE MORE RUINS BELOW US...AND ASHURA MUST'VE BEEN DRAGGED INTO THEM.
ASHURA... WHEREVER YOU ARE... HOLD ON!!

A VOICE... IT'S CALLING ME...
YASHA...?
NO...IT'S NOT HIM.
IT'S DIFFERENT...
THIS ENERGY WAVE IS MORE LIKE MINE.

WHOSE ENERGY WAVE IS THIS? IT'S NOT YASHA'S, BUT...
...IT FEELS LIKE THE SAME WAVE AS YASHA'S THAT PROTECTS ME...

NGH...

WHAT A STRANGE CEILING.
?

WHERE AM I?

WELCOME TO KUSUMAPURA...
...CHILD OF THE ASHURA.

I AM KUMARATEN, KING OF KUSUMAPURA.
I'VE BEEN WAITING FOR YOU, LITTLE LORD ASHURA.
...KUMARATEN...
YOU SAW WHAT REMAINS OF THIS ONCE-GREAT KINGDOM, CORRECT?

THE DECAY YOU SAW IS ALL THAT REMAINS OF A CITY THAT ONCE BOASTED TO BE THE RICHEST IN ALL OF TENKAI.
ITS NAME, THE FLOWER CAPITAL, CAME FROM ITS FLOWERS, WHICH BLOOMED THROUGHOUT THE YEAR...

BUT THAT AGE OF PROSPERITY ENDED WITH THE ANNIHILATION OF MY TRIBE...
...AT THE HANDS OF TAISHAKUTEN THOSE 300 YEARS AGO.
THE RUINS YOU SAW ARE NOT EVEN ONE TENTH OF THE ORIGINAL KUSUMAPURA.
I REMEMBER IT ALL TOO WELL... THE WRATH OF WAR BURIED MOST OF THE KINGDOM UNDERGROUND, ALONG WITH ITS INHABITANTS.
SOME WERE BURIED ALIVE...
...WOMEN AND CHILDREN WERE BURNT TO DEATH.
THE FEW WHO SURVIVED CURSED TAISHAKUTEN WITH THEIR LAST BREATHS.
BUT IT WAS ALL IN VAIN.
WHEN THE KILLING WAS OVER, KUSUMAPURA WAS LOST FOREVER.
HOWEVER...

...ALL IS NOT LOST.
I'VE BEEN HIDING IN THIS SUBTERRANEAN ABODE, WAITING FOR THE DAY REVENGE WOULD BE MINE...
THE DAY I DESTROY TAISHAKUTEN, THE GOD KING...
...AND AVENGE MY TRIBE.
LET GO OF ME!!
I WANT TO GO BACK TO YASHA AND RYUUY!
I'M SORRY... I CAN'T LET YOU DO THAT.
I NEED YOU TO REVIVE THE SHURA SWORD.
REVIVE... THE SHURA SWORD?
YES. THE SWORD CAN ONLY BE AWAKENED BY LORD ASHURA.
ONCE IT'S IN MY POSSESSION, I WILL BE ABLE TO DESTROY TAISHAKUTEN.
IT'S SPUN A COCOON AND I CAN'T GET NEAR IT. BUT YOU, ON THE OTHER HAND...

WITH THE BLOOD OF THE ASHURA YOU HAVE INSIDE OF YOU...I CAN BREAK THROUGH ITS BARRIER.
AND THE ECLIPSE THAT WILL OCCUR IN SEVEN DAYS' TIME WILL BE THE FINAL COMPONENT TO REVIVING THE SHURA SWORD.
I NEED TO BRING DOWN TAISHAKUTEN. AND TO DO THAT...I NEED YOUR BLOOD.
NO WAY!! YOU CAN'T DESTROY TAISHAKUTEN! YASHA IS GOING TO DO IT! HE PROMISED!
DON'T COME NEAR ME! I'M LEAVING AND THAT'S FINAL!
YOU LITTLE...!
YOUR LITTLE FIRE TRICKS WON'T DIVERT ME THAT EASILY!

GET BACK HERE!
AAAH!!

WATCH OUT!!
!
LORD ASHURA!!
......

RISKING YOUR LIFE FOR THE YOUNG KING...
YOUR DEVOTION IMPRESSES ME, KAHRA.

ARE YOU ALL RIGHT, LORD ASHURA?

I'M NOT GOING TO HURT YOU. AFTER ALL, YOU'RE GOING TO REVIVE THE SHURA SWORD.
UNTIL THE ECLIPSE, LORD ASHURA IS NOT TO LEAVE THE CASTLE.

LORD ASHURA.

PLEASE DO NOT WORRY. AS LONG AS I'M BREATHING...
...I WILL PROTECT YOU.
MY LIEGE.

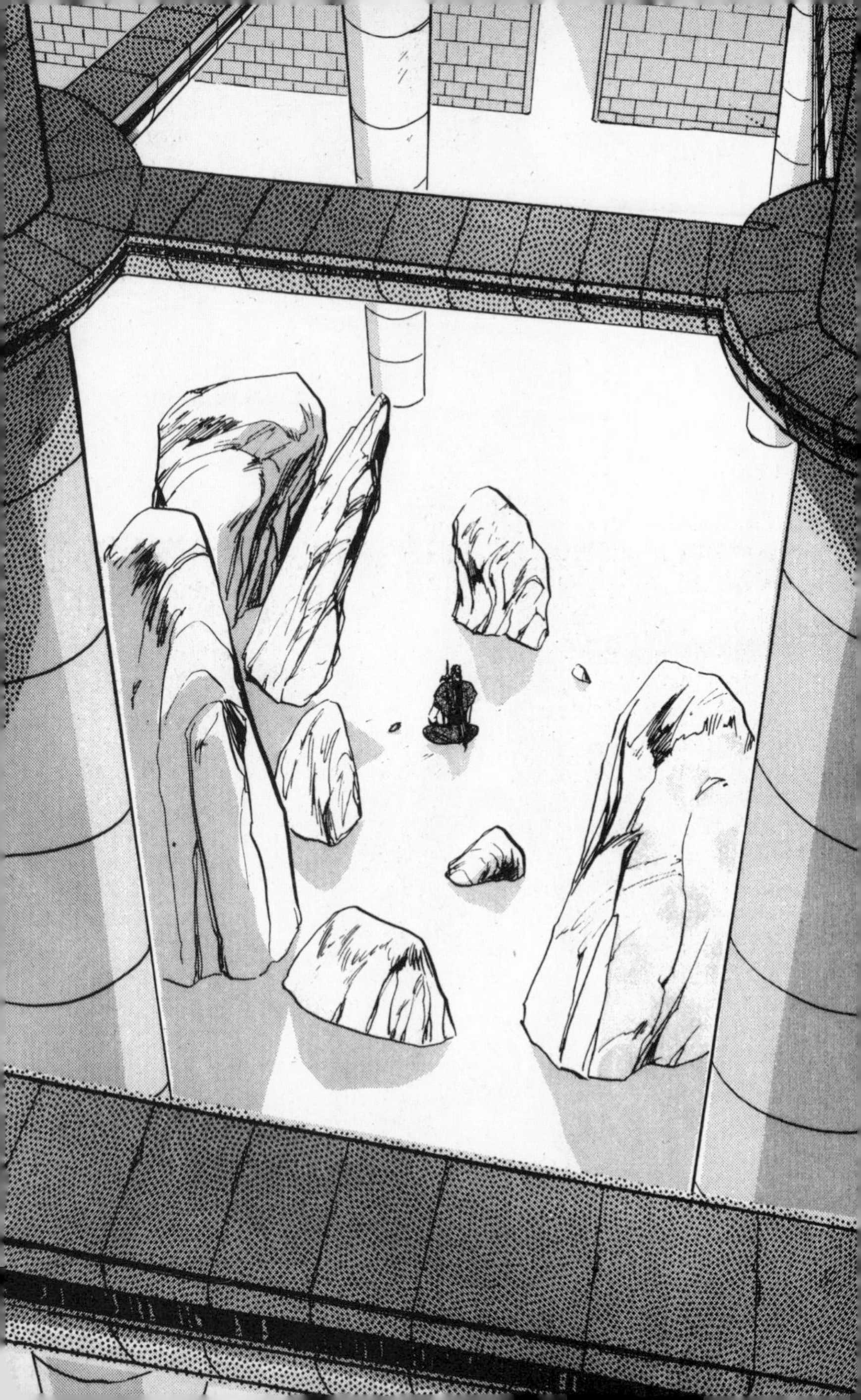

NO GOOD.
THERE'S NO ENTRANCE TO GO DEEPER.
BUT WHY WAS IT ONLY ASHURA WHO GOT PULLED DOWN? WAS THERE A TRAP DOOR OR SOMETHING?

SORRY, WRONG AGAIN!

WHO'S THERE?!

HOW DO YOU DO, YOUNG DRAGON KING?

I'M KUJAKU, THE WANDERING PLAYER!
BUT YOU CAN CALL ME "KU THE PLAYBOY"!

HOW COME EVERYONE KNOWS WHO I AM?!
ARE YOU ANOTHER ONE OF THOSE "HELP LORD YASHA AND PROTECT ASHURA" PEOPLE?
ぱたぱた
OH, NO NO. I'M MORE OF A "PLAYING CAT AND MOUSE WITH YASHA WITH ASHURA AS THE BAIT" KIND OF GUY.

KUJAKU, I WANT YOU TO TELL ME WHERE THE ENTRANCE FOR THE LOWEST LEVEL OF KUSUMAPURA IS...
...OR ELSE.
SORRY. ONLY KUMARATEN CAN OPEN THE DOOR TO KUSUMAPURA.
BUT DON'T WORRY. ASHURA'S DOING JUST FINE.
I MEAN, HE *IS* THE LORD ASHURA, AFTER ALL.
THAT MEANS HE'S FULLY CAPABLE OF TAKING CARE OF HIMSELF. HE'LL PROBABLY SHOW UP AGAIN, SHURA SWORD IN HAND AND EVERYTHING.

REALLY, LORD YASHA-- ASHURA'S GOT POWER THAT SURPASSES YOUR OWN. HE'LL BE FIIIINE.
Right? Right?
AS THE SAYING GOES, "IF YOU LOVE SOME-ONE, SET THEM FREE." SEE, EVEN LIONS EVENTUALLY KICK THEIR CUBS OFF A CLIFF TO GET THEM TO LEAVE HOME.
AND NO MATTER HOW MANY TIMES THEY CLIMB BACK UP AGAIN, AS RESPONSIBLE PARENTS THE LIONS KEEP KICKING THEM OUT--
THAT'S JUST PLAIN BULLYING.
しーん
DAMN... HE'S REALLY GLUM.
TELL ME ABOUT IT! HE'S ACTING LIKE HIS WIFE'S WALKED OUT ON HIM OR SOMETHING.
くるっ
THE ENEMY IS HERE!
I DON'T KNOW WHAT KIND OF BUSINESS HE HAS WITH A PILE OF RUBBLE LIKE THIS...BUT EITHER WAY, THAT LORD YASHA REALLY IS A FOOL.
Unbelievable! He moved!
Scaaary!
Crap, there he goes with his weapon again!

BLOCK ALL THE OTHER ENTRANCES!
I DON'T WANT EVEN A DRAFT TO GET IN!

PITIFUL REBELS. IN THE NAME OF MY MASTER KOUMOKUTEN, I, VARUNA, WILL CRUSH YOU!!
TEE HEE.
わき わき

FOOT-STEPS!
49...NO, 52 OF THEM!
Wow!
HERE COMES THE GOD KING'S ARMY!

LORD YASHA! THE GOD KING'S ARMY IS APPROACHING FAST.
UNDER WHOSE COMMAND?
THEY'RE WAVING THE FLAG OF KOUMOKUTEN, THE GENERAL OF THE WESTLAND. THERE ARE 52 IN TOTAL.

WHAT ARE YOU GOING TO DO, LORD YASHA? IT'S EITHER FIGHT OR FLIGHT AT THIS POINT.

ASHURA IS STILL DOWN HERE SOMEWHERE.

YOU SAID THAT SINCE HE'S REALLY *LORD* ASHURA, HE'LL RETURN, DIDN'T YOU, KUJAKU?

IS HE REALLY THE "KING"?
...
HE'S STILL SO YOUNG...
I WOULDN'T CALL 300 YEARS OLD "YOUNG."

50! 100!! I DON'T CARE HOW MANY, JUST LET ME AT 'EM! I'M ITCHING TO FIGHT!!
I'LL HELP YOU.
AND I'LL CHEER YOU ON!
HEY, LORD YASHA.
WHY ARE YOU SO INTENT ON PROTECTING ASHURA?
IS IT REALLY JUST TO GATHER THE SIX STARS AND DESTROY TAISHAKUTEN?
OR...IS IT SOMETHING MORE?

LORD ASHURA.
IS EVERYTHING ALL RIGHT?
NOTHING'S ALL RIGHT!
LET ME GO BACK TO YASHA! I WANT TO GO BACK! NOW!!

PLEASE WAIT JUST A LITTLE WHILE LONGER.
I'LL SEND YOU BACK WITH THE SHURA SWORD SOON. I PROMISE.
プイ
WHY SHOULD I TRUST YOU? YOU'RE FROM KUSUMAPURA, AFTER ALL... RIGHT, KAHRA?
NO... YOU'RE WRONG.
I WAS A PRIESTESS OF THE ASHURA.
I WAS THE ROYAL PRIESTESS TO THE FORMER LORD ASHURA.
A PRIESTESS...OF THE ASHURA?! I THOUGHT THERE WERE NO OTHER ASHURAS LEFT BESIDES ME.

SO THEN... THAT MEANS...
YOU KNOW ABOUT THE ASHURAS, RIGHT?
TELL ME ABOUT THEM!!
AS YOU WISH, SIRE.
THE ASHURAS WERE THE LIGHT OF TENKAI, WITH THE POWERS OF MAH-YAH AND FIRE.
LORD ASHURA WAS A GUARDIAN WARRIOR OF TENKAI. HE LED THE 12 GENERALS AND THE FOUR GODS WITH HIS STRONG SENSE OF JUSTICE.

THE ASHURA CASTLE WAS SISTER STRONGHOLD TO THE GOD KING'S ZENMI CASTLE. BUT MORE LIKE A REFLECTION IN THE WATER.
ITS MYSTERIOUS POWERS ALLOWED US TO LIVE IN ITS UNDERWATER DOMAIN.
ONLY THE ASHURAS AND THOSE SPECIALLY PERMITTED WERE ALLOWED TO ENTER.
KAHRA, TELL ME!
WHAT WAS MY FATHER LIKE?
A REGAL, STRONG, AND NOBLE KING OF THE ASHURA.
A TRULY GREAT MAN.
UM...AND, UH...
もじ
もじ
YES?
HOW ABOUT MY... MOTHER?

TELL ME ABOUT MY MOTHER, KAHRA.
WHAT WAS SHE LIKE?
ズギッ
UH... WELL...
I'D SAY...VERY INTELLIGENT AND ACTIVE, AND...
ぎゅっ
...VERY SKILLED IN ANYTHING SHE PUT HER MIND TO.
きちん
SHE WAS MY TWIN SISTER...AND HER NAME WAS SHASHI.
WE WERE BOTH ACCEPTED AS PRIESTESSES TO THE ASHURA. AS THE ASHURA TRADITION GOES, WE WERE HUMANS INDUCTED INTO THEIR TRIBE TO SERVE AS PRIESTESSES.
SHASHI... WHAT'S BECOME OF YOU?

IT FEELS LIKE I'M DREAM-ING.
I STILL CAN'T BELIEVE WE WERE CHOSEN TO BE THE PRIESTESSES OF THE ASHURA...
KAHRA...
WHAT ARE YOU TALKING ABOUT?
I THINK WE'RE SKILLED ENOUGH TO QUALIFY AS MORE THAN JUST PRIESTESSES.
DON'T SAY SUCH A THING, SHASHI...
IT'S ANY HUMAN'S DREAM TO BE ABLE TO WORK FOR LORD ASHURA.
WHAT'S MORE, WE RECEIVED THE POSITIONS OF ROYAL PRIESTESSES, AND EVEN THE SAME LIFE SPAN AS THE OTHER HEAVENLY GODS--
THEN IT'S NATURAL FOR A PRIESTESS TO BE TREATED AS A GOD.
SHASHI...
WE'RE DIFFERENT, YOU AND I.

I WON'T BE SATISFIED JUST BEING A "PRIESTESS" OF THE ASHURA, SISTER.
I HAVE A WISH, YOU SEE. AND THAT IS TO STAND ABOVE EVERYTHING AND HAVE EVERYONE KNEEL AT MY FEET! NOT ONLY HUMANS...
...BUT ALL THE GODS OF TENKAI, TOO. EVERYTHING IN THE WORLD!
SHASHI, LISTEN TO YOURSELF! IT'S AWFUL FOR A HUMAN TO HAVE SUCH A WISH!
NO, *YOU* LISTEN.
I'VE ALREADY RECEIVED THE POWER TO MAKE MY WISH COME TRUE. LORD ASHURA GAVE IT TO ME.
THE POWER OF A GOD AND THE SAME LIFE SPAN, TOO.

BEAUTIFUL, STRONG AND SCARY SHASHI...MY TWIN, BUT THE COMPLETE OPPOSITE OF ME.
ピィ
ピィ
OH, SHASHI, WHAT A CHARMING BIRD!
I GOT HER FROM THE KING.
YOU CAN HAVE HER, KAHRA.
WHAT? BUT HE GAVE HER TO *YOU*...
WELL, I'M A BUSY WOMAN AND YOU'RE NOT. SO YOU TAKE CARE OF IT.
SHASHI WAS CHOSEN TO BECOME THE QUEEN...
...AND MARRIED LORD ASHURA.

THE QUEEN HAS SPOKEN.
NOW, LOOK AT THIS! WHAT DO YOU THINK OF MY WEDDING DRESS?
OH.
WHAT DO YOU THINK YOU'RE DOING TO MY GOWN?!
STUPID BIRD!
NO, SHASHI! DON'T!!

CLEAN UP THIS MESS, WOULD YOU?
ぐすっ
SHASHI GOT MARRIED TO LORD ASHURA...
...AND SOON AFTER, SHE WAS PREGNANT WITH THE KING'S HEIR.
THAT'S YOU.
BUT THEN, DURING THE HOLY WAR 300 YEARS AGO...

I SUMMON YOU, RAGO, THE GUARDIAN BEAST!
SHASHI!
WHERE ARE YOU GOING?!
TENKAI IS IN TROUBLE! YOU HAVE TO DO SOMETHING!!
YOU...YOU'RE THE QUEEN, AREN'T YOU?!
WHERE ARE YOU GOING AT A TIME LIKE THIS?!
SILLY, SILLY KAHRA. DON'T YOU SEE THAT THIS IS THE PERFECT TIME TO MAKE MY WISH COME TRUE?
I'M LEAVING.

STOP! DON'T GO TO TAISHAKUTEN!!
STOP DECEIVING LORD ASHURA AND YOUR PEOPLE!
OH, SO YOU KNEW ABOUT US ALL ALONG, EH?
IF YOU REALLY MUST SEE HIM, PLEASE PROMISE ME THAT THIS WILL BE THE LAST TIME.
AT THIS RATE, NO MATTER HOW MANY HUNDREDS OF YEARS HE FIGHTS, TAISHAKUTEN DOESN'T HAVE A CHANCE OF WINNING!
THAT'S RIGHT...AT THIS RATE.
BUT IF SOMEONE FROM THE ASHURA HELPED HIM, IT'D BE EASY FOR HIM TO CONQUER TENKAI.
SOMEONE WHO KNOWS EVERYTHING ABOUT THE ASHURA'S ARMY. THEIR WEAKNESSES, POTENTIAL...EVERY-THING. SOMEONE LIKE...ME.
I COULD CARE LESS WHO WANTS TO BECOME THE GOD KING...
...AS LONG AS I GET TO STAND BY HIS SIDE AS HIS WIFE.

HE NEVER LOOKED AT ME AS A REAL WIFE.
HE ONLY SAW ME AS A MEANS TO AN HEIR.
I'D RATHER BE THE WIFE OF THE KING OF TENKAI THAN THE WIFE OF SOME MEASLY GUARDIAN WARRIOR.
SHASHI! WAIT!
DON'T YOU LOVE LORD ASHURA?!
WHAT ABOUT YOUR BABY?! THAT BABY IS LORD ASHURA'S!!
ダッ
HMM, THAT'S TRUE...HE MAY BE A GLITCH IN MY PLANS...
I SUPPOSE I'LL JUST HAVE TO TAKE CARE OF IT...LIKE THAT BIRD THE OTHER DAY...

I'LL KILL IT WITH MY OWN HANDS.
KAHRA? HEY!
WHAT WERE YOU GOING TO TELL ME ABOUT MY MOTHER DURING THE HOLY WAR?
OH! UH...
THERE WERE SOME DIFFICULTIES. SHE COULDN'T BRING YOU UP THE WAY SHE WANTED TO...
BUT SHE WAS REALLY LOOKING FORWARD TO YOUR BIRTHRIGHT FROM THE START.
REALLY ?!

THERE YOU ARE, KAHRA.
OLD ONE...
KUMARATEN WANTS TO SEE YOU. GO IMMEDIATELY.
TSK. THAT AIRHEAD PRIESTESS... ALWAYS WASTING TIME...
WHAT'S HIS PROBLEM?! COME ON, KAHRA, YOU DON'T HAVE TO TAKE ORDERS LIKE THAT FROM KUMARATEN!
WHAT A DESPICABLE MAN! I HATE HIM!
DON'T SAY THAT, ASHURA. HE REALLY IS A GOOD MAN.
TRUE, HE'S GOTTEN A LITTLE TWISTED WITH HIS GRUDGE AGAINST TAISHAKUTEN.
BUT DEEP DOWN, HE HAS A GOOD SOUL.
KAHRA...DO YOU LIKE KUMARATEN?
THE TRUTH IS... I'M EXPECTING A BABY.
AND THAT BABY...IS KUMARATEN'S.

WOW! REALLY?! CAN YOU FEEL THE BABY INSIDE YOU?
......
THIS BABY SHOULDN'T BE BORN.
A BABY NO ONE WANTS...
HOW CAN YOU SAY THAT?! THAT'S A HORRIBLE THING TO SAY!!
THAT POOR BABY!

IF ONLY YOU DIDN'T EXIST... I WISH YOU WERE DEAD!
GIGEI SAID SHE NEEDED ME!!
SHE SAID... I'M NEEDED.
IT HURTS WHEN PEOPLE SAY THEY DON'T NEED YOU. IT'S SAD TO BE AN UNWANTED CHILD.
YOU CAN'T GO ON LIVING IF NOBODY NEEDS YOU.

KAHRA.
WHAT TOOK YOU SO LONG?
IT APPEARS THAT NOW THAT YOU'RE BACK WITH YOUR *REAL* MASTER, YOU DON'T PAY MUCH ATTENTION TO THE TIME.
HMM. GET OVER HERE.
AH!

YOU'RE LOOKING A LITTLE PALE. ARE YOU FEELING ALL RIGHT?
ARE YOU WORRIED ABOUT ME?
O-OF COURSE NOT! DON'T JUMP TO CONCLUSIONS!
I'M JUST WORRIED ABOUT...
...THE BABY.

THAT BABY IS GOING TO BE KING OF THIS UNDERGROUND CASTLE AFTER ME.
YOU'RE JUST A PRIESTESS OUT OF WORK. OF COURSE THE BABY COMES FIRST!
KUMA-RATEN...
MY MOTHER WAS LOOKING FORWARD TO MY BIRTH.
THAT'S WHAT KAHRA SAID.
I'M *NOT* AN UNWANTED CHILD.
THIS IS THE FIRST TIME I'VE BEEN APART FROM YASHA FOR SO LONG. I WONDER HOW HE'S DOING..
YASHA... COME FIND ME, PLEASE...

HA HA HA HA HA!
WHAT SAD EXCUSES FOR OPPONENTS YOU REBELS MAKE! NOT WORTH EVEN A SECOND OF MY MASTER'S TIME!
I'LL SAVE HIM THE TROUBLE AND BRING HIM YOUR HEADS!!
WAH HA HA HA HA
TA DAA

YOU'VE GOT A BIG MOUTH, YOU KNOW THAT?! YOU'RE NOT COMING NEAR MY PEOPLE!!
I GUESS THAT MEANS THE DRAGON TRIBE HAS TURNED AGAINST THE GOD KING TOO...
TRAITORS DESERVE NOTHING BUT DEATH! AND WITH YOU OUT OF THE WAY, I'LL BECOME GUARDIAN WARRIOR OF THE WESTLAND!
OH YEAH?! WE'LL SEE WHOSE HEAD ROLLS FIRST!!
OHO! SO, THE DRAGON KING HAS ALSO JOINED THE REBEL CAUSE, EH?
I'LL GIVE YOU A QUICK DEATH WITH YOUR HEAD AS MY REWARD...AND SAVE THE FUN FOR WHEN I FIND THAT DEMON CHILD.
NOW, LORD YASHA. HAND OVER THAT ASHURA KID. I KNOW YOU'RE HIDING HIM.
SAVE YOUR BREATH, DRAGON SCUM!
HOLD YOUR TONGUE IF YOU WISH TO SAVE IT.
GYA HA HA HA HA
HA HA HA HA!
THE "STRONGEST GUARDIAN WARRIOR IN TENKAI" CAN'T PROTECT HIS OWN TRIBE...AND NOW NOT EVEN A LITTLE CHILD!! PATHETIC!!

WHA... WHAT'S THAT AURA?!
HIS EYES... THEY'VE TURNED DARK RED!!

OH GOOD, THE FUN'S STARTING! ♡
FOR HIS EYES TO CHANGE FROM DARK BLUE TO BLOOD RED... I DON'T EVEN ***NEED*** TO GUESS HOW ANGRY HE IS.
IF YOU'RE OUT TO CLAIM MY HEAD...
...JUST GO AHEAD AND TRY IT.
BUT I WILL ***NEVER*** LET YOU TOUCH EVEN A SINGLE HAIR ON ASHURA'S HEAD.

I-it's a monster!
MEN! STAND YOUR GROUND!
JUST WHAT KIND OF POWER IS THIS?!
THAT AURA'S GOT US ALL TRAPPED UNDER ITS SPELL...
FINALLY, I GET TO SEE IT!
フォオオオオオ
SO THIS IS THE TRUE POWER OF THE KING OF THE YASHA...
THE POWER OF LORD YASHA, THE FIERCEST GUARDIAN WARRIOR OF ALL!!

YAMA!
どひーっ
GYAH!
IT'S HIS
DEATHBLOW...

HEAVENLY WOLF BLADE!

GYAH!
OH BOY... THAT WAS SOME-THING.
Holy...
H-HOW... DARE YOU...

LORD YASHA, YOU BASTARD!! I'LL MAKE YOU PAY DOUBLE FOR THAT!!
That really threw me...but only for a moment. (Varuna)
YOU! TAKE CARE OF THE LITTLE DRAGON KING AND THAT WOMAN!
YES, SIR!
LORD YASHA IS MINE...AND THE ASHURA KID WILL BE, TOO.
OOOOH BOY! HE SAID THE "A" WORD AGAIN...
THE MORE HE SAYS "ASHURA," THE MADDER IT MAKES LORD YASHA...YOU KNOW?

Jerks!
LITTLE?! WOMAN?! WHO DO YOU THINK YOU'RE TALKING TO?!
I'll kill ya!
NOW, NOW...
GIVE HIM NO MERCY! JUST KILL HIM, LORD YASHA!!

I'LL TAKE CARE OF HIS LACKEYS!! BUT SAVE THE HEAD OF THAT GOON VARUNA FOR ME, GOT IT?!
LORD RYUU...
...THAT KIND OF TALK WILL HURT YOUR GOOD-GUY IMAGE.

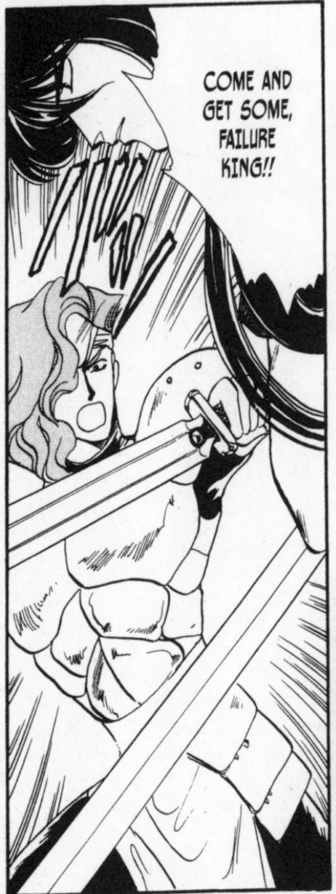
COME AND GET SOME, FAILURE KING!!

WHAT'S WITH THE HESITATION? DON'T YOU REALIZE IT'S AN HONOR TO END UP A BLOODY SMEAR ON THE DRAGON TOOTH SWORD?

HA! THAT SWORD'S ALL BARK AND NO BITE!
HOW DO YOU EXPECT TO CHOP US UP WITH SUCH A BLUNT WEAPON?! DON'T MAKE ME LAUGH!!
"BLUNT"? THAT'S IT, NOW I'M MAD! SOUMA, LET'S TEACH THESE BASTARDS A LESSON IN MANNERS!
HIYAAAAAA!!
I'LL CUT OUT YOUR TONGUES AS A SAMPLING!
TWIN MOON LEAVES FLY!

AAAGH!!
AGH!
EVIL
SEA DRAGON
WAVE
CRUSH!!

GYAAAHH!
AAAH!

I ALWAYS HATED THE RUMORS THAT THE YASHA TRIBE BOASTED THE STRONGEST SWORDSMEN IN TENKAI.
YOU'RE JUST COUNTRY FOOLS! THE SWORDPLAY OF THE NORTH IS NOTHING LIKE FIGHTING IN THE REAL WORLD!
WHY COULDN'T I BE A GUARDIAN WARRIOR? I'M FAR MORE QUALIFIED THAN YOU!!
WELL, LORD YASHA?!
HERE'S MY CHANCE!
He's completely open!
GOT YA!
WATER ILLUSION BLADE!!

Damn!
HE...HE BLOCKED IT USING ONLY HIS LEFT ARM!
THIS ISN'T GOOD!
AGH!!
Aaaahh!

THAT ALL YOU GOT, VARUNA?
FIRST YOU THREATEN THE LIFE OF MY CHILD...
...THEN YOU TREAD ON THE NAME OF MY TRIBE?
I'LL MAKE YOU PAY FOR YOUR POMPOUS ATTITUDE.
I DON'T TAKE SUCH ABUSE LIGHTLY.
WHATEVER YOU DO, IT WON'T MAKE ANY DIFFERENCE.
EVERYONE IN TENKAI KNOWS...
...YOU'RE THE WORST KING EVER.

BY PROTECTING THAT ASHURA KID, KNOWING FULL WELL THE DANGERS OF DOING SO...
だらだら
...YOU'VE CURSED YOUR ENTIRE TRIBE TO DEATH! YOU'RE A JOKE OF A KING!
I GUESS THAT CHILD WAS IMPORTANT ENOUGH TO RISK YOUR PEOPLE. I HOPE YOU ENJOY YOUR TIME TOGETHER IN THE NEXT LIFE, TOO!!
LISTEN HERE! I AM VARUNA, THE WATER GOD!!
YOU...
AND I'M SENDING YOU STRAIGHT TO HELL!!
HOW DARE YOU SAY HIS NAME, "ASHURA," SO CASUALLY! FILTH!!

PLUTO'S DESTRUCTION, SLAY ILLUSION!!
WAAH!

WHAT'S THIS LIGHT?!
STORM OF THE SIX STARS PART 1 / THE END

RG
聖
伝
VEDA

PRESIDENT
HO HO HO HO HO HO
OH
I'LL HAVE EVERYONE KNEEL AT MY FEET! THE PRESIDENT, THE CHIEF...EVERYONE!
Second secretary
First secretary
SOB SOB
SHASHI ...
RG VEDA BONUS MANGA

THE 12 GENERALS' ROOM
That's right!
WHY DOES OUR BOSS HAVE TO BE MARRIED TO SUCH A BITCH?!
The nerve of her!
WHAT'S *WITH* THAT WOMAN?!

SHE WAS SWINGING HER GOLF CLUB IN THE OFFICE THE OTHER DAY.
I'm gonna hit a driving range on the way home from work!
OH HO HO HO HO
Here!
SHE CAN'T MAKE DECENT TEA, SO SHE ALWAYS LEAVES IT UP TO THE EXECUTIVES.
I SHOULD SEND HER MY KNUCKLE PUNCH!
I can't believe our president drew straws to choose his bride... what a lazy-ass.
One for all, all for one!

HEY, BOYS!
ぐいーっ
ごくごくごくごくごくごくごくごくごく
WATCH THIS!
ぷはーっ
SOMEONE GET ME SOME PRETZELS!
どん!

BY THE WAY, HERE'S THE KEY TO A BENZ. I FEEL LIKE GOING HOME BY BENZ TODAY. SO WHO WANTS TO BE MY BENZ?!
Name of the horse
I'M SO SORRY, NORASION!
It looks great on you!
AH HA HA HA HA
What the hell is this?
SHE PUT A ROLLS ROYCE HOOD ORNAMENT ON THE NOSE OF MY HORSE YESTERDAY.
I'LL NEVER LET YOU BE HER CAR! NEVER!
SOB SOB
BENZ
GA HA HA HA HA
UNDEFEATABLE
I THOUGHT I TOLD SOME-ONE TO GET ME PRETZELS!!
SHASHI, THE STRONGEST CHARACTER IN RG VEDA! SHE DOESN'T SEEM TO HAVE A CLUE WHAT'S GOING ON BUT SHE CAN ALWAYS LAUGH HER WAY OUT OF A SITUATION! TAISHAKUTEN, ARE YOU SURE YOU WANT TO STEAL HER FROM LORD ASHURA?! I WONDER WHAT RG VEDA WOULD BE LIKE IF IT WERE ALWAYS SET IN AN OFFICE..
STAY TUNED FOR THE NEXT EXCITING EPISODE OF RG VEDA BONUS MANGA!!
▼ Taishakuten from the Promotions Department

CLAMP NEWSPAPER

PIRATED EDITION RG VEDA BY MICK NEKOI

......
I'm out of the panel...

THIS IS THE PIRATED EDITION OF RG VEDA.
Why am I Kujaku?
I'm happy...

NOW, I'D LIKE TO EXPLAIN CLAMP TO THE READERS WHO ARE READING THIS MANGA FOR THE FIRST TIME.

CLAMP IS...

...A GROUP OF FOUR PEOPLE WHO ARE FROM OSAKA, KYOTO, AND SHIGA.

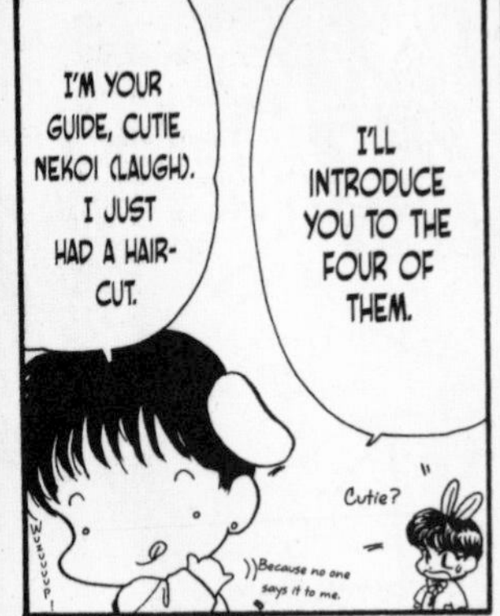

I'LL INTRODUCE YOU TO THE FOUR OF THEM.
I'M YOUR GUIDE, CUTIE NEKOI (LAUGH). I JUST HAD A HAIR-CUT.
Cutie?
Because no one says it to me.

THIS IS AGEHA OHKAWA, THE LEADER OF CLAMP. SHE WRITES THE ORIGINAL STORY, EXPEDITES THE PROCEEDINGS, PRODUCTION, LAYOUT, ETC. SHE DOES A LOT OF STUFF.
WU-ZUUUUP!
AGEHA OHKAWA

WE OFTEN GET QUESTIONS LIKE "WHY IS SHE THE ONLY ONE WHO'S DRAWN BETTER THAN THE OTHERS?" AND "IS SHE MAKING YOU DRAW LIKE THAT?"...BUT THAT'S NOT THE SITUATION. I'M JUST EXAGGERATING HER CHARACTERISTICS.
She works in an outfit like this.
ACTUALLY SHE PREFERS A SIMPLE DRAWING LIKE THIS.

NEXT UP, MOKONA. SHE RECEIVES THE ORIGINAL STORY FROM AGEHA OHKAWA AND CREATES THE STORYBOARD AND THE ARTWORK.
WU-ZUUUUP!
MOKONA

SHE TAKES AN ACTIVE PART IN OUR WORK, LIKE BEING THE MODEL OF CLAMP'S MASCOT CHARACTER.
THAT HAS NOTHING TO DO WITH IT, DOES IT?

SHE NEVER PUTS ANYTHING AWAY. THAT SHOWS YOU HOW FOCUSED SHE IS ONCE SHE STARTS TO WORK.
SHUT UP!!
Just kidding! Moko-chan is a good, hard-working girl.

THIS IS SATSUKI IGARASHI. SHE RECEIVES THE ART AND DRAWS PANEL LINES, AND APPLIES SCREEN TONES.
WORD.
SATSUKI IGARASHI

SHE DOES A LOT MORE JOBS. ONCE IN A WHILE, SHE'LL DO SOMETHING STUPID, BUT BESIDES THAT, SHE'S A PRETTY COMPETENT PERSON.
I wanna eat crabs...
AND SHE'S A GREAT COOK.
THOUGHTFUL, TOO.
DON'T FORGET SHE EATS A LOT.

WHAT'S GOOD ABOUT EATING A LOT?
SHE FINISHES THE LEFT-OVERS.
BUT IF SHE'S NOT IN THE MOOD TO EAT, SHE COULD GO ALL DAY WITHOUT A BITE.
Hey, are you guys really trying to help?

I'M TSUBAKI NEKOI. I DRAW THE SIMPLE BACKGROUNDS, ACTION LINES, APPLY SCREEN TONES, AND FINISH UP THE ART WITH SATSUKI.
WU-ZUUUP!
TSUBAKI NEKOI

I MAKE THIS CLAMP NEWSPAPER.
SHE EATS A LOT, TOO.
SHE EATS THREE TIMES A DAY.
WHY ARE WE STILL TALKING ABOUT THIS...?

SO, WE FOUR CREATE THE ART OF CLAMP.

BY THE WAY, CLAMP HAS JUST MOVED.

THIS IS THE 5TH TIME SINCE WE CAME TO TOKYO TOGETHER.

OUR NEW PLACE HAS A ROOSTER DOWNSTAIRS AND HE CRIES REALLY LOUDLY IN THE AFTERNOON.

WE DID A GOOD JOB ON THE INTERIOR DESIGN THIS TIME.
It's a big problem to put away all my stuff.
I never know what's where in your room. It's a miracle you can fit such a lot of stuff in there.

CLAMP NEWSPAPER *COCK-A-DOODLE-DO*

I WAS USING A FUTON BEFORE, BUT I PURCHASED A BED THIS TIME.
THE BED IS FILLING UP HALF OF YOUR ROOM...
Oh, a close-up.

I'D LOVE TO GET MORE NEW FURNITURE, BUT IT'S EXPENSIVE.
But I bought a chest made in Romania.
I'M INTO CHESS THIS YEAR, SO I BOUGHT A SMALL CHESS TABLE. IT'S CUTE.
Right now "Alice's Chess Set" is on it. I have a Disney chess set, too.
I'll collect more.

I'M REALLY INTO THE MENU FROM "SKY-LARK", NEAR OUR PLACE.
WHAT ARE YOU TALKING ABOUT?
"SKYLARK" HAS LOTS OF GOOD THINGS ON THE MENU. CLAMP RECOMMENDS THEIR "TUNA TATAKI MEAL." "THE CRAB MEAL" IS VERY GOOD, TOO.
Buttered corn is good, too.
I LIKE "LOTTERIA'S" ICED TEA. IT'S GOOD.

WE HAVE A JAPANESE RESTAURANT NEAR US. IT'S REALLY GREAT.
But I won't tell you the location.
WE'RE ALWAYS EATING! WE'LL PUT ON WEIGHT!
YEAH!
Crabs...
Because that's the only fun we have.
Just kidding.
Tee-hee.

BY THE WAY...
WE HAVE SOMETHING IMPORTANT TO TELL YOU.
ぱかん

AS YOU KNOW, CLAMP WAS PUBLISHING AN INFORMATION MAGAZINE CALLED "CLAMP LAB," BUT WE STOPPED IT IN APRIL, 1994.

AS THE NEWS AND NEWSPAPERS SHOW, THE POSTAL FEE IS GOING TO CHANGE OFFICIALLY. WHEN THAT HAPPENS, WE HAVE TO CHARGE MORE FOR THE MAGAZINE SINCE WE'RE PUBLISHING IT WITH A LIMITED COST.

THAT'LL MAKE PEOPLE WHO KINDLY BUY CLAMP'S BOOKS AND CDS PAY MORE.

SO, "CLAMP LAB" WILL CONTINUE UNTIL APRIL 1994, BUT CLOSES AFTER THAT.

SO, RIGHT NOW WE CAN'T TAKE ANY MORE SUBSCRIPTIONS.

"CLAMP LAB SECRETARY ROOM", THE TELEPHONE SERVICE, WILL CONTINUE AS ALWAYS.
Script

WE'LL DO OUR BEST TO GET YOU ALL THE INFORMATION THROUGH "CLAMP LAB SECRETARY ROOM."

THANK YOU FOR YOUR UNDERSTANDING.

"Storm of the Six Stars" was published in "Wings" 1-6 edition in 1990.

"CLAMP LAB SECRETARY ROOM" IS USING THE REGULAR PHONE LINE, SO YOU CAN LISTEN TO IT ANYWHERE IN JAPAN.

AS IT'S A TELEPHONE SERVICE, YOU CAN RECEIVE THE NEWEST INFORMATION ABOUT CLAMP FASTER THAN ANY OTHER MEDIA.

THE INFORMATION IS RENEWED TWICE A MONTH—THE 1ST AND THE 15TH.

CLAMP LAB SECRETARY ROOM

WE'RE PLANNING TO GIVE A PRESENT JUST FOR PEOPLE WHO LISTENED TO "CLAMP LAB SECRETARY ROOM". PLEASE LOOK FORWARD TO IT.

"CLAMP LAB SECRETARY ROOM" IS RUN BY CLAMP. PLEASE DON'T CALL SHINSHOKAN TO INQUIRE ABOUT IT.

I didn't have a very big part...
I'm dressed up!
RG VEDA WILL CONTINUE FOR A WHILE. WE'LL BE VERY HAPPY IF YOU SUPPORT IT!
Oh ho ho ho ho.
HAVE A NICE DAY

NEXT TIME IN RG VEDA

YASHA CONTINUES TO BATTLE HIS WAY TO ASHURA IN KUSUMAPURA...BUT HIS JOURNEY TO FIND THE SIX STARS WON'T END THERE. DESTINY WILL LEAD HIM TO THE SKY CASTLE, THE DOMAIN OF QUEEN KARURA... WHERE TRAGEDY AWAITS.

COMING SOON!

that I'm not like other people...

FROM THE ARTIST OF SUIKODEN III

BY AKI SHIMIZU

QWAN

Qwan is a series that refuses to be pigeonholed. Aki Shimizu combines Chinese history, mythology, fantasy and humor to create a world that is familiar yet truly unique. Her creature designs are particularly brilliant—from mascots to monsters. And Qwan himself is great—fallen to Earth, he's like a little kid, complete with the loud questions, yet he eats demons for breakfast. In short, *Qwan* is a solid story with great character dynamics, amazing art and some kick-ass battle scenes. What's not to like?

~Carol Fox, Editor

BY KEI TOUME

LAMENT OF THE LAMB

Kei Toume's *Lament of the Lamb* follows the physical and mental torment of Kazuna Takashiro, who discovers that he's cursed with a hereditary disease that makes him crave blood. *Lament* is psychological horror at its best—it's gloomy, foreboding and emotionally wrenching. Toume brilliantly treats the story's vampirism in a realistic, subdued way, and it becomes a metaphor for teenage alienation, twisted sexual desire and insanity. While reading each volume, I get goose bumps, I feel uneasy, and I become increasingly depressed. Quite a compliment for a horror series!

~Paul Morrissey, Editor

STOP!

This is the back of the book. You wouldn't want to spoil a great ending!

This book is printed "manga-style," in the authentic Japanese right-to-left format. Since none of the artwork has been flipped or altered, readers get to experience the story just as the creator intended. You've been asking for it, so TOKYOPOP® delivered: authentic, hot-off-the-press, and far more fun!

DIRECTIONS

If this is your first time reading manga-style, here's a quick guide to help you understand how it works.

It's easy... just start in the top right panel and follow the numbers. Have fun, and look for more 100% authentic manga from TOKYOPOP®!